SHINE HOW TO SURVIVE AND THRIVE AT WORK

CHRIS BARÉZ-BROWN

PORTFOLIO PENGUIN

Published by the Penguin Group

Penguin Books Ltd, 80 Strand, London WC2R 0RL, England

Penguin Group (USA) Inc., 375 Hudson Street, New York, New York 10014, USA

Penguin Group (Canada), 90 Eglinton Avenue East, Suite 700, Toronto, Ontario,
Canada M4P 2Y3 (a division of Pearson Penguin Canada Inc.)

Penguin Ireland, 25 St Stephen's Green, Dublin 2, Ireland
(a division of Penguin Books Ltd)

Penguin Group (Australia), 250 Camberwell Road, Camberwell,
Victoria 3124, Australia (a division of Pearson Australia Group Pty Ltd)

Penguin Books India Pvt Ltd, 11 Community Centre,
Panchsheel Park, New Delhi – 110 017, India

Penguin Group (NZ), 67 Apollo Drive, Rosedale, North Shore 0632,
New Zealand (a division of Pearson New Zealand Ltd)

Penguin Books (South Africa) (Pty) Ltd, 24 Sturdee Avenue,
Rosebank, Johannesburg 2196, South Africa

Penguin Books Ltd, Registered Offices: 80 Strand, London WC2R 0RL, England

www.penguin.com

First published 2011

2

Copyright © Chris Baréz-Brown, 2011

Set in Hadrian and Century Schoolbook

Printed in Italy

ISBN: 978–0–241–95234–4

To my wife, Anna.

Nobody has ever inspired me to be more. You are a constant revelation, never settling for less than extraordinary. I am blessed to have met you, let alone married you. A more Elvis chick couldn't exist. Bring on the next adventure!

THE SHINY STUFF

SHINE BRIGHT

Work is a huge part of who we are.

Not only does it give us money to live, it shapes our most important life decisions: where we live, who our friends are, the time we spend with our families.

Work can define how we see ourselves, often wrongly. It consumes enormous amounts of our time, energy and focus.

The much-used motto of the working populace is: 'I don't live to work, I work to live'.

That doesn't add up.

If you work full time you probably spend at least forty-five hours a week at work, more than ten hours preparing for and travelling to it, countless hours recovering from it … and weekends thinking about it.

Surely, in order to live life to the full, you must love your work too. You have to create some impact, be yourself and shine as brightly as you can. Otherwise it would be a huge waste of life. You'd just be taking up space.

Work is designed to trap us. It is complex and devious.

It is hard to even notice the trap – which is why so many of us fall into its clutches.

There is always the next thing to strive for. Few ever see the bigger picture; most see only next week. When we are young, most of us take on mortgages that keep us focused on paying off a twenty-five-year debt; this is hardly conducive to taking creative risks and breaking the rules.

The grand plan keeps us busy and keeps our heads down, rarely giving us a glimpse of what could be. Of what we could be. Before long we are shaped by what is around us and not by possibility. Our fears make us play safe and play the game. So many people die without achieving their dreams, settling instead for just comfort and security.

But it doesn't have to be this way. Work can be the most rewarding aspect of our lives. It can make us grow, nourish us and even entertain us. It can connect us to worlds we can only dream of and reward us with an enviable lifestyle. It can be stimulating, exciting and fun.

Work can be the best game in town. The question to ask yourself is: 'How can I be better at playing that game?

WAKE UP!

WHO'S ELVIS AROUND HERE?

Bono, the lead singer of U2, is one of the world's best known advocates of human rights. When he goes into any organization as part of his well-publicized mission to eradicate Third World debt, the first question he asks is: 'Who's Elvis around here?'

It's a fabulous question.

The Elvis Bono is looking for is the person who stands out, breaks the rules, makes things happen, shines more brightly, and probably loves every minute of it.

I believe everyone can be a bit more Elvis. Everyone has the ability to stand out.

Imagine that every day you could jump out of bed, loving what you are about to do, excited by the game you are going to play, and knowing that you can only win. That's a very powerful place to be, and provides more laughs per minute than most people experience in a week.

Shining brightly can manifest itself in all business activities. It could be the way you run meetings.

It may be that when you interview someone, you try to ensure that the interviewee learns and grows through the process rather than just responds to your questions. It might be that every time you walk through reception, you spread a little happiness and humour.

The manner in which you shine is down to you. The only essentials are that shining should be fun, human and engaging, and that you put a little of your unique magic into the business.

Shine is for everyone who wants to shine brighter at work.

This book is an alarm call. It is shouting: 'Wake up!'

You can work to live and be ordinary, or you can live through your work and be both extraordinary and fulfilled. The only limitation is you: your energy, your belief, your perspective.

By playing with *Shine* you will learn how to be a bit more Elvis and how to get a bellyful of the laughs that are on offer at work.

Bring it on …

UNDERSTAND THAT YOU ARE AMAZING

You are incredible.

You can process information faster than any computer on the planet.

You can replicate cells and heal yourself.

You are so sensitive to information and the world around you that you can perceive molecules in the air and small changes in light and movement.

You have mastered language and can interact with others without even trying.

You have the ability to think freely and express who you really are.

You have no limitations but the ones you impose upon yourself.

You have all you need to shine bright.

CHOOSE TO STAND OUT

Shining isn't compulsory. If anything, the opposite is true.

Society certainly won't encourage you to shine; it will do its best to make you fit in, small and unnoticed. Business needs its worker ants, those who turn up every day and toe the line, head down, never challenging the status quo. Most managers will admit that it's harder to manage Elvises. The talented ones are too much for a mediocre manager to bear, as they constantly strive to improve standards.

So there is plenty of space for you to carry on in this world without causing ripples, without being noticed, and no one will object if you do.

But there is another option. You can be you. All of you.

You can be that extraordinary human being that you have always known lies deep within you.

You can decide that it's time for the real you to cast off the shackles you have been using to define yourself, and shine in all that you do.

You can stand tall, take a huge bite out of this life and savour the taste.

The choice is yours.

Why aren't you making it?

If you are scared, what are you scared of? What can really go wrong?

If you are lazy, take a good look at the person you'll become if you don't change.

If you don't know how, read this book. And if you just don't want to change, then why did you buy it?

ABUNDANT THINKING

Our minds are highly efficient killing machines. They are trained from an early age to destroy anything that doesn't fit our model of the world.

Recent research suggests that as few as 28 per cent of the world's potential breakthrough ideas (a cure for Alzheimer's, the wheel, McDonald's value meals) have been discovered so far. If true, this is almost certainly a result of our analytical and reductionist style of thinking.

Just consider that for a second.

What's going through your mind? Are you questioning how things might have been different today if all those amazing ideas had been thought of, and asking whether we can do something about it?

Or are you asking who did this research? What is it based upon? What is the definition of a breakthrough idea?

If you're in the first camp, I believe you have a chance to make more of a difference in this world and certainly in business. Far too many people live their lives in the second camp, because we have been trained to do so very effectively for so long.

This means analytical, logical minds dominate our working lives. If a colleague brings us a new perspective, insight or idea the trigger in our minds delivers 'combat thinking' before we can even be conscious of it. If this new view has weak defences, our minds will find a way in and destroy it.

Jo, a talented innovator I have worked with for years, was once media director of Saatchi Australia. She went on a negotiation training course with the rest of the board. It was run by a pair of British ex-army officers who had been trained in negotiation skills for hostage situations, so it promised to be a fun day.

In one exercise she was asked to pair up with the finance director (for maximum drama). They were placed at the front of the room with everyone watching. An orange was placed in front of them and they were both given a piece of paper with their instructions. They were told to read them and then negotiate possession of the orange.

Of course they did what everyone tends to do and tried charm, cunning, bribery, mild threats, feigned disinterest and humour in their attempts to make the other person concede the spoils. Then, as usual, when all else failed they stopped and read the instructions. The light bulb went on: Jo's script said she needed the orange to make juice. Mike's said he wanted it to make marmalade.

They could each have what they wanted from the same orange, and would have reached that conclusion more quickly if they hadn't jumped to the immediate conclusion that the only way to achieve their objective was to beat their opponent.

Our logical, analytical brains naturally make us assume that what we have seen happen before will happen again, and lead us to play out our lives on autopilot. Abundant thinking breaks that cycle by helping us to consider futures that are not based on past experience.

In this case their combative thinking led to combative actions of the type that so often fracture our energy and that of our potential partnerships. By thinking abundantly, the exercise would have been nailed in seconds.

New perspectives are just stimulus.

We don't have to be scared of them.

They can't hurt us. We decide what to do with them. There is no need to react in a 'kill or be killed' fashion just because a new perspective has been shared with us.

Next time your mind goes Rambo, take notice. Step back and observe what causes the violent reaction and how quickly it goes from one kill to another. Then breathe, smile, sit straight and notice how the killer can become a puppy: playful and interested in all the things around you.

When you embrace abundant thinking you soon realize that people want to be near you.

You shine more brightly and sprinkle possibility in places where surprising results may appear.

Such a small mental change can transform an interaction, meeting or team into a force for good in the world.

FILTERS OF FANTASY

We all have good days and bad days. Wouldn't it be great if we got to choose which one rather than just playing the hand we are dealt by the gods?

Some days at work, you feel bulletproof. Nothing can stop you from having a fantastic day and even if it rains on the outside, you feel sunny on the inside. If your boss is in a bad mood, you find it funny. If Finance sends back your expenses with a query you think, 'Good on you, guys; that diligence means this business is safe,' and when your PC crashes for the fifteenth time you think, 'I am sure those tech guys are doing their best and there is a great reason we can't have Macs.'

On other days we are not so robust. The toner is gone on the printer again and you want to resign. ('This place sucks, you are all losers, I am rotting away in this hell hole, pass the Scotch!')

In both situations, you are the same person. You have the same skills and talents, and yet you're experiencing two very different days or even two very different realities. That's because your head is creating two very different states in you.

Your 'state' is simply my term for 'how you are' at any given point in time; it dictates how you perform and how much fun you have. State is constantly changing in subtle ways depending upon external stimulus and internal processing; mostly we are unconscious of its influence, but every now and again we can't help but pay attention.

For example, you've had a great year and in your review your boss gives you a maximum bonus. In this case your head says, 'Fantastic, I'm valued, recognized, my efforts were worthwhile, I belong here!' That creates a state where for the rest of the day it's likely you are going to have a great time, because the emotional resonance is so high.

If the boss had expressed a different view of you and your delivery, and said that you had performed poorly and that this year your bonus was keeping your job, your head might be saying, 'I hate you and everyone else, you must think I am rubbish, I've obviously been a laughing stock all year.'

THE WAY THIS WORKS IS:

TRIGGER (IN THIS CASE, YOUR BOSS'S VIEW OF YOUR PERFORMANCE)

FILTER (YOUR INTERPRETATION OF THAT VIEW)

STATE (HOW YOU ARE AS A RESULT)

So what's important about this process?

Firstly, we can't control our triggers and nor should we. Life should be dynamic and surprising; if we waste our energy like Howard Hughes trying to protect ourselves from the outside world we have missed the point.

So there will be triggers in our lives that affect our state both negatively and positively, and hallelujah for that. Those rich emotions are called life.

The challenge, however, is that at times our state is so stuck that a quick-fix cup of tea, chat to a mate or walk round the block won't get us into a place that is more useful and fun. The key to making that change is to understand our filters.

Our filters are interpretations of the world.

They happen so fast that we are largely unaware of them and yet they drive our behaviour and how much we enjoy our business life. They dictate how effective we are in business and how much we shine. In the two examples of how we could react to a trigger (an annual review), notice how different our filters are. Your review changes nothing that has happened during the past year, but what your boss says can create two radically different interpretations and therefore reactions.

The reason they are so different and wildly resonant is this: often, the filters in our heads have nothing to do with the reality of a situation. Therefore we can put the most fantastical and ridiculous interpretations on events, which then produce negative reactions. The stuff in our heads could be absolute rubbish, and yet we regard it as the gospel truth.

Stop the knee-jerks

I have experienced this myself. I was once told by one of the 'guv'nors' of my last business that creativity was 'low rent'.

This is what happened in my head instantly: 'I believe creativity is important, he thinks it's low rent, therefore I must be low rent, which means my work won't be valued. I am therefore wasting my time and I should resign and do something else.'

I know that sounds laughable, but when I go back to that moment and ask why I felt so bad, that's what I hear in my head.

Of course, it's all rubbish. Deep down I know that creativity is vital, and that if we were all to embrace it, the world would be truly extraordinary. But at that moment I had a different perspective: a negative, out-of-control, spiralling-down perspective. The reason my reaction was so powerful was that the comment was about me and what I stood for, and it was delivered by my boss, someone I respected and who is a great friend.

His intention was not to upset me; in fact, quite the opposite. He had a point of view that he thought could be useful for me in my work. I then used it to upset myself and have a thoroughly miserable day. Well done, me!

Think how often this happens to you. How many times have you misinterpreted the actions or comments of colleagues and consequently reacted in the wrong way? This is the human condition. It is designed to protect us from risk. In the past it could have been life-saving. Unfortunately, in today's business world it takes away our shine and leads to negative knee-jerk reactions in situations that could indeed be of positive benefit.

When you realize that you are having a negative reaction, stop, breathe, sit or stand straight and notice what is going on inside you.

Your state will have changed, but the question is, what's going on in your head? Slow it down to grab hold of its tail; when you do so you will see the whole beast and all the filters that created it. You can only slow it down by stopping and breathing and becoming aware of what's happening to you.

The more aware you become of these filters, the more choices you have about how you want to be. The more choices you have, the better you are ... and the brighter you shine.

SLOW DOWN

Business runs fast, and business wants more. We run fast, and we want more. The world is spinning so quickly that just to keep your feet connected to its surface is a huge achievement.

Yet fast and more are not great. We think they are because they make life exciting. When we are busy we feel as though we're achieving something and we feel as though we are important. The truth is very different: if you are too busy and too hectic you lose your impact and your shine.

To truly shine, you need to tune yourself into you, the people around you and the context in which you work. To do that you need to slow down and take a deep breath. Literally. By breathing deeply you feed your brain more oxygen, which it needs to function well. It then begins to relax and connect to your subconscious.

In this state you can make better connections, flex perspectives and be more open to possibilities. You can explore opportunities that will only be viewed as distractions when working too fast on too much.

Avoid stimulants. Avoid multitasking. Avoid saying yes to others when you want to say no.

Be ruthless with your time and then give generously with absolute attention when you do share it.

Sit straight, breathe and smile and notice how connected you are to you, to the people around you and the context in which you work.

I used to run the marketing for Grolsch lager. There was intense pressure to plan lots of brand activities: a bit of TV, some posters, magazine ads, in-store and on-pack promotion, launch some new pack types, extend the brand, PR, sponsorship, new bottle design, sampling, trade incentives, bar-staff T-shirts, etc. etc. etc.

It all sounded great and would keep me busy with lots of activity all year. Gosh, how we like busy.

Truth was, all we needed to do in one particular year to get good growth was sort out trade pricing, get the pack

SLOW
DOWN!

strategy right and run a few press/poster ads for some awareness. It was all done in the first quarter, which left lots of time to think about big ideas for the future.

Beware of being too busy. It dilutes you.

It may feel good, but it's not where genius lives.

Genius needs space and time to reflect, different stimuli and free-wheeling interactions with interesting people. Cut the crap and be brilliant every day.

PERCEPTION FLIP

There is no such thing as truth or reality, only perception.

That's a big concept, but the more work I do in business, the more evidence I have to support it.

Even the absolute measures that we have created are anything but absolute. Talk to any creative finance director and you'll know what I mean. For instance, a company is only worth what someone will pay, and that is their perspective of its value.

If perspective is everything, you need flexibility and awareness in how you perceive.

Make the distinction between a good perspective and a stuck one.

A good perspective means trying on many viewpoints to find the one that best fits you at that moment. Good perspective is driven by the ability to be sensitive enough to each view that you can choose the best one in the circumstances.

If you can select a perspective that works for you, you can also choose the way you want to be: energized, angry, passive, melancholy, or on a mission to spread joy. Your perspective delivers how you are; how you are will then deliver the results you need.

Try this out. List ten reasons why your life is looking fantastic right now. Any reasons at all, as long as they give you some energy. Do it standing up. And say them out loud, not just in your head or scribbled on a pad.

How do you feel?

Nothing has changed in your life and yet you feel so much better. Your blood pressure has dropped and you've created some cool pictures in your head. No doubt you are smiling.

This is a far more useful state from which to shine in business. You are energized, positive and dynamic. All you had to do was to change your perspective.

Every day we have the opportunity to choose perspectives. We can select perspectives that take our power, make us victims and keep us small, or the ones that are entertaining and exciting and make us huge. You choose.

BE HUMAN AND SCREW UP

Business is a human pursuit, yet so often we become someone else when we go to work. We believe that there is a type of person who gets on here, a type different from who we really are, and we pretend to be them. It is almost impossible not to.

Such 'schizophrenia' may be found in any organization, no matter how creative or cool, as we all have a strong drive to conform if not consciously then subconsciously. This is partly because we learn by emulating and partly because we are conditioned not to stand out from the crowd, but by doing so we lose a lot of our uniqueness.

To shine, we have to reclaim who we are.

A simple way to do so is to show more of our humanness and to let go of what is often perceived as professionalism.

That means showing our struggle, our screw-ups and our downright stupidity.

We all have flaws, so let's not pretend that we are perfect little business soldiers.

I'm not saying that we shouldn't care or that we should adopt a sloppy attitude; quite the opposite. In fact by being more human we tighten up our understanding of what 'great' looks like.

When we show a bit more of who we are, people find it endearing and will connect with us more easily, helping us shine more brightly.

This is particularly true when presenting to a group.

If you are too slick, the human connection is harder to establish.

The most engaging people share their foibles and get things wrong, but then work with it.

The classic story of valuing cock-ups has become a thing of legend. A man working for a bank invests tens of millions of the bank's money in a property development that goes bump. He goes to his boss with the intention of resigning. His boss says, 'I don't accept your resignation: I have just spent millions of dollars on your development, I now want to see it pay off!'

If only we all had such an enlightened approach to experiments going wrong.

Often we can use a failure to our advantage. Cock-ups appeal to human nature, so come clean and use them as opportunities.

When the Kellogg's manager who disastrously changed the name of Coco Pops to Choco Krispies left the business, the team decided to right the embarrassing wrong. They felt it had been a bad decision made for reasons of management control, and wasn't in the interests of either the brand or its customers. Kellogg's hoped that if they changed it back people would forgive and forget.

However, rather than doing so quietly and apologetically, the team decided to celebrate the situation. They ran an election-style TV advertising campaign inviting their customers to vote for their preference. Almost one million people responded by telephone and online. Coco Pops were once more and volume sales went up 80 per cent.

The campaign has influenced Kellogg's marketing ever since. Screw-ups create energy, and energy can always create opportunities.

GO WITH THE FLOW, UNLESS ...

You possess only a finite amount of energy, as does your business. You can use your reserves to fight against the flow of the business energy in an attempt to change it, or you can use it to your advantage and move with it.

I am a huge fan of laziness. Why swim upstream when I can float downstream? It's far more pleasurable and all I have to do is find value in a different destination. At least when I get there I have the energy to make the most of it. So go with the flow.

Use the company structures, systems and initiatives to your advantage and your efforts will be better rewarded. If you feel that your work life is a struggle, ask how it could be made effortless.

To be lazy, you have to be smart. Use energy only where it is needed. Only go against the flow when doing so is iconic; then the substantial energy you use will give you even more energy back.

Constantly trying to change everything is exhausting and rarely results in much. Go with the flow instead.

For example, if you are passionate about encouraging more creativity in the business but you can't get things going, take a look around and see whether you can use what's already there. What values are in the business, what key strategic initiatives, leadership skills, goals? How can you use them to help you get where you want to be?

A friend of mine was once on holiday in the beautiful Balearic Islands. In his vacation mode a rush of blood to his head made him swim out from the shore so he could body surf the crashing waves. As he paddled onto his first wave he was dumped with all the might of the ocean into what he later described as a washing machine full of foam.

Regaining his dignity, he found his feet and managed to unsteadily make his way back up the beach. He reached to his head in search of his brand-new £500 prescription Ray-Bans. Of course, they were gone. That rush of blood was proving to be rather expensive.

Feeling like a chump, he sat in the sand gazing out to sea. As he did so he noticed a small piece of driftwood in the waves and saw that the currents were slowly bringing it to the shore. This gave him an idea.

He swam back out to the waves where he had been dumped, and just starting floating, allowing the sea to bring him back to shore. He had realized that the movement of the waves was the key to finding his precious eyewear. Within minutes he saw the glasses on the sea bed below him.

What he had done, quite intuitively, was to go with the flow. He could have spent days searching hopelessly, but by harnessing the flow the task became surprisingly easy.

What would be the equivalent in your business life? Is there something that you've been struggling with against the tide? If you were to go with the flow you might get a much better and more pleasurable result.

Find a wave that helps you, and ride it.

FIND A WAVE
THAT HELPS YOU,

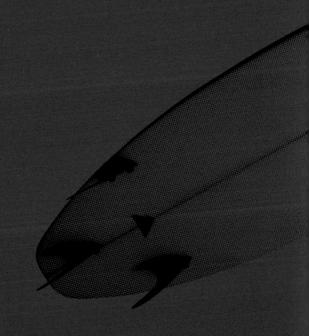

AND RIDE IT.

PERSPECTIVE PRACTICE 1: YOU AREN'T YOU

Every day, you're a different person. When you wake up, you spend the first moments remembering who you are.

When you wake up tomorrow, choose to emphasize facets of yourself that you really value. Then see how things change. For example, when you wake, choose to be deeply interested in everyone that you meet that day, or perhaps amused by the ridiculousness of accepted business practice.

Close your eyes, breathe, visualize that.

Try a few on.

Which perspectives give you more energy? Which give you less?

If a perspective gives you more, live with it for a bit and try it on. It may become part of your wardrobe.

KNOW WHAT YOU STAND FOR

Things change because people care. There is no point trying to have a big impact on something that is meaningless to you. Why would you bother? We also have a need for focus. Without it we don't function well – our brains are less efficient and our energy becomes dispersed. So we have to choose carefully where to invest our time.

To really stand out, we have to know what we stand for. History is littered with people who have achieved extraordinary things because they had no choice. Geldof and Gandhi believed so adamantly that they must change the world, so they just had to.

The Sultan's Elephant

One of the most spectacular events I have ever seen took place in London in 2006, when the centre of the capital was sealed off so that a 40-tonne elephant could be paraded through

its heart. The elephant in question was the Sultan's Elephant, a twelve-metre-tall puppet created by French artists Royal de Luxe, and over one million people came to see it. The show had an incredible effect: people were crying in the street, overcome by emotion. It was nothing like a typical London day.

After the terrorist bombings in July 2005 London had become highly policed. The idea of shutting the streets for a work of art sounded crazy; but not to Helen Marriage. She was the producer of the event through her company, Artichoke, a visionary who believed passionately in bringing the remarkable spectacle to the people of London. When she agreed to take on the project, however, the Metropolitan Police, Buckingham Palace, the Royal Parks and London Transport had all refused permission for it to go ahead.

Undeterred, she eventually managed to persuade all the relevant authorities and bring the city's commercial centre to a halt, all with a core team of four. It was a monumental achievement.

On a typical weekend Oxford Street is visited by over a million people and is the scene of many arrests. The same number came to witness the Sultan's Elephant and the police arrested no one. London was touched.

Time stood still. An extraordinary moment happened all because one woman stood up for something that she really believed in. London shone a bit brighter because of Helen Marriage.

Although there were many talented people involved in making the event happen, David Aukin, Chair of Artichoke, gives us a sense of why she achieves what she does: 'Helen is exceptional, and not only because she makes it impossible to say no to her. She has the gift not only of making you believe anything and everything is possible, but then also of proving that it is.'

The good fight

These days, it's all too easy not to care about anything very much at all.

Life is easy. Most of us have all we need to succeed and thrive in comfort. In the developed world, few are hungry, cold or homeless unless by choice or catastrophic circumstance. Few are exposed to the really dark side of human nature or plumb the very depths of despair. Most of us live our lives on autopilot and wrapped in cotton wool.

What is seen on the news can seem as unreal as a Hollywood film. Our headspace for soul searching is limited because we fill every moment with stimulus so we hardly ever hear what's inside. We keep our minds busy by flitting from one indulgence to another, or one job to another.

No wonder there are fewer rebels these days. What is there left to fight against?

Plenty. I believe there are many things we should all feel strongly about, things we can stand for, things that would make the world a better place. I am not talking about lofty causes like banishing famine or war, but the principles behind those actions, such as fairness and humanity. They are in us all, but are often anaesthetized by the hamster-wheel of society.

What's important to you, important enough to fight for, important enough to make a stand?

What have you read that has created a real reaction in you?

What have been the real highs and lows of the last year, and why?

What was it that created such resonance in you?

Are you passionate about learning and growth, trying new things, diversity? Do you feel challenged by exciting stimulation, collaboration, or risk taking? Do you love the arts in business, or helping others discover their talents?

You can be motivated by anything that gives you energy and helps you make a mark on the world in a unique way.

How can it be linked to what you do every day?

Once it is, you will have the power of stampeding elephants and the belief that changes the big stuff. Make it happen.

PEOPLE NEVER HAVE THEIR BEST IDEAS AT THEIR DESK.

DOWN WITH DESKS

A desk can be a useful place for getting stuff done. Desks are designed for ergonomic efficiency and the physical support they provide helps get that analytical and logical brain of yours working in a laser-like fashion. To do a good job you need that.

But people never have their best ideas at their desk. When I ask people where they've been most inspired, the answer might be walking the dog, driving, in the shower, in bed, in the pub, playing golf, running, on the train … but never at their desk.

Getting out of the office creates a different state in you, which means you can access more of your brain. More brain means more processing and more rich stimulus, delivering better ideas.

It's vital to vary your working day. I used to work in a business that didn't have enough space for us all so we spent slugs of time working in cafes and bars. It was one of my most creative periods as I always had a changing environment (not to mention cheap office space and coffee on tap).

GO SOMEWHERE ELSE. DO SOMETHING THAT HELPS YOU RELAX AND OPENS YOU.

Always leave your desk for lunch, and regularly get off-site. I tend to find that forty-five minutes is long enough to stay in one spot, so I habitually move after that time. You don't have to climb Machu Picchu for creative inspiration; any movement or change is useful.

So next time you need breakthrough thinking, don't sit at your desk trying harder. All that will happen is that you will get less creative as your limpet-like brain attaches itself to the rock of reductionism.

Go somewhere else. Do something that helps you relax and opens you. There's a whole world out there full of possibility. Go bathe in it.

NOTICE WHEN OTHERS ARE GREAT

I once heard a famous businessman speak, and he told how his father became a different person depending on whether he was working for his big-company employer by day or in his own grocery store at night. By day he was lethargic, browbeaten and under pressure. At night he came alive, loving the detail and the routine of being his own boss in a small business. Even the

difficulties he faced in the store were treated as special moments.

I have experienced the same thing. As an employee I'd have great weeks and average weeks. However, my performance, good or bad, went pretty much unremarked upon until it came to my annual review, by which point if I was miles off target we could have just wasted twelve months. Equally my great performances often went unregistered too.

Since working for myself, everything has changed. I now own my performance, because if I don't, my business is likely to fail.

I am not alone in this experience. Everybody I have spoken to echoes the same thing. I fundamentally believe that employment is bad for people. Yes, I understand that it means that we have predictability and security and we can plan our lives. I also understand that it means that business leaders can plan and use their resources and talents in a more efficient way.

However, when somebody knows that they will receive the same reward for a great week as for a terrible week, a part of them dies.

Their subconscious realizes that the extra effort that they could make will give fractional reward, and that cutting corners, if smartly done, will have no repercussions. No wonder that there are so many people who just turn up for work and count the minutes until they can go home again. At home they can do something that they love, they are in control of and naturally recognized for.

Make it personal

If you really want a shiny business, make sure you notice when the people you work with are great. And appreciate them for being so.

Ideally, their daily salary would rise or fall depending on how well they have done. In most businesses, such a system would be almost impossible to implement, but what you can do is make sure that people feel they are rewarded for their effort on a weekly basis.

It doesn't have to be all about money, it's about making sure that you recognize when they do well and when they don't. You need to acknowledge when they go the extra mile or take a risk, when they've learned something valuable by doing something different, when they have tapped into their genius and shined more brightly.

Some of the most potent rewards I have seen have been the most personalized, and the cheapest.

Handwritten letters are often treasured for years. One company had a stuffed animal called Bernard that sat on the desk of anyone who had been spotted doing something great. Anyone could nominate a colleague for anything they valued – gaining a million-pound contract, bringing in a home-made cake – so the idea was self-policing; Bernard could be on your desk for mere seconds before moving off. It sounds nuts and yet I heard members of the board whingeing that they hadn't had Bernard for a while so they had better pull their fingers out.

Without such a grasp on how your people are performing it is all too easy for them to become zombies, the working dead, the ones who show up in physical form only.

Personally, I want the magical people working for me. So notice when they're great and then make sure that they know you noticed.

747 HEAVEN

Travel is a business necessity. Technology means we don't have to do as much of it these days, but there is no better way to build a relationship than face-to-face. So no matter how eco-friendly we are, we still need to get on planes sometimes.

There are lots of downsides – jet lag, airline food and being away from loved ones – but there are also some fantastic upsides.

There is something wonderful about the cocoon that you find yourself in at 36,000 feet. I have had some of my best ideas at altitude and I know I am not alone. My phone doesn't ring and I can't be bothered by e-mail unless I want to. But more than that, there seems to be an increased sensitivity to stimulus.

I remember flying back one Friday evening from Moscow. There always seem to be older planes on that route, which is appropriate, given the rather red-nosed older male passengers usually found in business class. There was little choice when it came to entertainment, but after a hard week's work most people seemed happy to watch the classic that is *Cheaper by the Dozen 2*.

I went to the front of the cabin to use the facilities and to stretch my legs. On returning to my seat I noticed that half of the passengers had tears streaming down their faces. Although Steve Martin's comic genius is renowned, these were tears of emotion rather than laughter.

It is anything but a sad film, but at 36,000 feet our emotions are heightened and we feel a lot more than we ordinarily do. There are no distractions and therefore we can have surprising reactions to not only the entertainment but also our own thoughts.

This is a wonderful resource to have. I know people who book business trips just so they can get a new perspective on projects they are working on or some significant aspect of their lives.

I have a little rule for long-haul flights. No work after the main meal. I get to the departure lounge early and clear everything so that I can relax, enjoy the peace and allow my mind to wander. Bliss.

If we have to travel, let's use it to make sure that our Elvis is well and truly upped.

KNOW YOUR NORTH STAR

One of the most frustrating questions I ever used to hear in interviews is: 'Where do you see yourself in ten years' time?' Who has a clue? Life is so dynamic, changing so fast, that to know what we are doing next week ain't bad.

You do, however, need a North Star, something to direct your actions on a daily basis. The North Star can change as you change and as your environment changes. But it's important to know where you're moving towards: what kind of life you want and what kind of person you want to be. It is the quality of vision that is more important than its precision.

Those people who can only be fulfilled with a ranch in Montana, a Playboy bunny wife and a dog called Ace are unlikely ever to live the dream. If, however, their dream is to live in the countryside, have a partner who is fun to be with and to spend time with animals, there will be a far better chance of success.

Fundamentally, visions are only icons of the life we

would like to lead, so the trick is to understand what those icons represent for you.

Every day we have to make hundreds of decisions. We need some type of compass to help us decide whether they are the right ones or the wrong ones. In truth there is no such thing as right and wrong, there are just some actions that are more directionally appropriate than others. Your North Star is there to guide you when making decisions. It should help you become the person you want to become and enjoy the journey rather than the ultimate destination that needs to be reached for happiness to be yours.

I used to hate having goals and visions, because to me it meant I had only one option. The truth is, your goal is purely for today, for now. Tomorrow, when you wake up a new person, you can tweak and change and recalibrate depending on who you then want to be.

As life develops, so do those goals. Don't see them as limiting; see them as emerging and ultimately energizing. If at work you don't know where you're going, chances are you're just warming a seat. All of us need to know if we have had a great day or not; without understanding that, how will we ever achieve all that we can?

One of my good friends has a great way to keep pushing his perspective. He collects articles, quotes, stories and pictures that make a big impression on him. He puts them into a scrapbook that he reads every couple of weeks. He then relaxes and lets his mind wander as this stimulus spins in his head. Invariably he feels inspired and often has new and different ideas while staying close to what he cares about. He ensures that his mind is fed by what he wants and not what society dictates. This stimulus acts as his North Star and is a powerful yet simple method any of us could use.

Ponder where you are going and what achievements are important to you. What is special about those goals? What will it mean to you if you reach them?

An Aston Martin will not make you happy. It may give you pleasure, but happiness comes from inside.

So which journey is going to help you achieve the most?

IF AT WORK YOU DON'T KNOW WHERE YOU'RE GOING, CHANCES ARE YOU'RE JUST WARMING A SEAT.

ASSUME EVERYONE IS AN ANGEL

Try this. Assume that the intent of your colleagues is good. Most often you will be proved right. If you assume positivity, life is Technicolor. If you look for crap, that's what you'll find.

We all need a break, a reminder about how fabulous we are. When someone naturally assumes that we are shiny, bright and fantastic, that's what we go back to: our original state.

We are easily warped in the moment, but our true nature is to have fun. See that in all and that's what will show up in every experience you have. In effect it creates your reality.

Every interaction is a chance for you to see the sparkle, the Elvis in others. Knowing all their variety of behaviour makes life a richer experience; everything that angers you can also help you learn.

Watch people who are stuck, send them love. When they send you bad things, enjoy the hilarity. When you can't understand how this could be good, laugh.

Assume positivity and feel your liberation begin.

We all get people asking us for career help. It may be an overt 'give me a job' meeting, or something more tangential, but if you are into people it naturally happens.

My brother Mark is a founding partner in Weapon 7, a London-based integrated marketing agency, so he gets approached for 'a little chat' all the time. He tries to see everyone who asks to see him, even if for an hour over a coffee. People have told him this is a waste of time and shouldn't be a priority, even when he makes it one. But Mark believes that anyone could have what it takes, regardless of their CV and experience; and if they don't fit now they could at least grease the wheels for his company in the future. After all, nice brings nice.

One man, Tom, was so impressive that Mark promised to employ him as soon as a vacancy arose. The very next day one of his team resigned. Tom was immediately offered the post and they were working together within five weeks.

If Mark hadn't assumed everyone is an angel he would never have discovered the huge talent that is Tom.

REST

To be great business bunnies, we need a great deal of energy. We can exercise, watch what we eat and sleep like a baby; however, there is a key to making sure that energy reserves are at a higher level. Rest.

In modern business we undervalue rest. Rest looks a bit ineffectual, a bit weak. When Nike hit a challenging period some years ago they put temporary beds in staff offices and launched a rousing battle cry: 'sleep when you are dead'. That mentality still fans the flames of our competitiveness and can be useful when used tactically. The problem arises when it becomes de rigueur in the business culture.

The idea of sitting at your desk reading a novel would be alien to most in business. Yet at times it's exactly the right thing to do.

I know many business leaders who regularly nap or meditate during the day. They are senior enough to do so and they see the value in topping up their energy reserves. Most of their staff would feel disloyal and lazy if they were to do the same. Most people work, decompress and then sleep. Decompression is often quite a busy experience. It can involve doing household chores, drinking, filling our heads with more stimuli such as watching TV, meeting friends or even doing some more work. None of those are truly restful.

Resting involves doing very little. A gentle stroll, playing some relaxed guitar, reading a book, taking a long hot bath. It helps us to regenerate physically, mentally, emotionally and spiritually. Good rest has little agenda.

EXAMINE YOUR WEEK AND SEE WHETHER YOU CAN PINPOINT THOSE TIMES THAT **YOU TRULY REST.**

IF IT'S NOT HAPPENING EVERY DAY, **DIARIZE IT** NOW (IN A SUPER RELAXED STYLE, OF COURSE).

GIVE YOUR MEETINGS TEETH

I know there are productive meetings in this world, ones where things happen. But most meetings are wholly inefficient and a terrible waste of time. Meetings are like a black hole that sucks people's hope, energy and talent into it.

There are countless reasons why these little get togethers are so ineffectual, but for a quick fix try to focus on these two underlying points. Firstly, concentrate on how they are managed; secondly, make sure the right people are there.

The management of any meeting is absolutely critical. It's something that even the most senior managers seem to struggle with, yet running one efficiently is largely a matter of common sense. Here's a simple checklist to make sure you are on track:

Before the meeting, make sure that everyone knows what the purpose of it is, and its vision of success. Sometimes meetings are purely for exploration, which is fine as long as everyone knows it. Many meetings are successful only if decisions are made about what happens next, which requires a different structure and outcome from a creative kickabout. If you are clear about the purpose of the meeting, running it becomes much easier.

Make sure the environment in which you hold the meeting is appropriate for the topic. If it is all about budgets and agreeing numbers, then huddling around the table and looking at some charts on PowerPoint is probably OK, but any meeting that involves exploration, creativity, or true interaction needs space and light and air and the things that make us tick.

I always take tables out of meeting rooms. A room containing only chairs gives people nowhere to hide and tends to create a more awakened state. Some meetings are even best held standing up: short, punchy and to the point. Make sure the environment creates the right conditions for the work you're doing. A one-on-one brainstorming meeting might produce better results if you're walking in the park.

If you hold regular meetings, make sure they don't always take place in the same location, otherwise the comatose state of the attendees from previous meetings will be re-triggered as soon as they enter the room.

Make sure that there is some magic designed into the agenda. To get the right balance to your meeting you need to appeal to the attendees' hearts and minds. It's one thing to be aligned to output that's core to the business strategy, but it's quite another thing for them to be excited about devoting their time to you and your agenda. If you sprinkle some pixie dust into a meeting by doing things in a different way, by bringing in interesting stimulus, by making the whole thing fun, then you will get far more from every head in the room. When working on a project to improve the customer experience of a bank, I decided to experiment with two approaches. First, we discussed it and launched into a good old traditional logical debate about the issue and what could be done. It was painful and got us nowhere apart from the land of frustration.

The second tack felt different: we started not by talking but by drawing. That alone helped us to see things differently. We then shared personal experiences of when we felt really well looked after in life. We left the building together and went to look at a few banks, but also hotels, restaurants and even casinos to see how they looked after their customers. By the time we got to thinking about how to make things better, we were stimulated from several sources. The ideas started flowing. The second approach was much more successful, because everyone was more engaged and had a different view of what could be done.

Agenda items

When you start the meeting, remind people about its purpose, and personalize your vision of success so it really feels like it's something worth doing.

Do introductions. These shouldn't take for ever – we don't need to know everyone's life history, but we do need to know who's in the room and why. Watch out: the more senior the person, the more embellishments and emotive description they are likely to include. Manage them.

Set out agenda and timings. Short is best. It's easier to manage energy and focus. I like forty-five-minute sections that are punctuated by something different such as a change of location, topic or facilitator.

Beware of all-day meetings. Rarely do our agendas perfectly fit a day. They either have padding or are too busy. Think very carefully about what is essential and make that the focus.

Watch out for those agenda items that would just be 'nice to do'. We aren't great at multiple deliverables. If we need to make decisions, that should be the focus;

if we need to just hang out more, make that the design.

We can't concentrate for a day, so design 'logic sessions' next to 'reflective sessions' next to 'creative sessions', and keep it moving.

Set out the behaviours you want from people in the meeting and agree them. Make it fun and human and you will get more back.

Leave no doubt that you are in charge. There can only be one leader at any given point. You may delegate others to run sections within the meeting, but you've got to be the captain of the ship.

Begin on time. If you don't, the start to the meeting is floppy, and if it starts that way it will continue that way. Nothing drives me crazier than weak time management. If you can't manage your own time and diary, a simple and finite resource, best not give you any complex responsibilities like budgets or people.

When closing, let everyone know what's changed as a result of the meeting. If nothing has changed, the meeting was a waste of time.

Finish early and debrief. Emphasize not what has been decided, but how the meeting went and what could be done to make it even better next time.

Meetings often waste talent and hope because the

wrong people are there. Only allow into the meeting anyone who will substantially contribute the content and/or decision-making. If ten people attend, they can't have more than 10 per cent airtime each, which means eventually they start to shut down and their subconscious can then become mischievous. Small is beautiful; everyone then has to be involved.

If anyone turns up to your meeting with an entourage, ask them to leave. If they can't add value themselves, they shouldn't be invited.

If the purpose of the meeting is enrolment or communication, ask whether there is another way of doing that. If you have meetings during which some of the time is spent making decisions or having ideas and some of it spent making sure that everyone buys into those actions, I would suggest you already have a messed-up agenda. Do one thing, and do that thing well.

I have known people who have wasted a large chunk of their business life squatting in meetings.

'It's a place I can hide, a place I can relax. It's lovely to hear what other people have been up to and every now and again all I need to do is say something smart and the coffee and buns just keep coming.'

Many professionals spend far too much of their business lives in meetings, giving them little time to deliver their agreed actions and even less to do their real jobs.

Only attend meetings if there is a clear agenda, you know your role and it seems like fun. Unless you have brought a duvet and some hot chocolate and are counting the days till your pension.

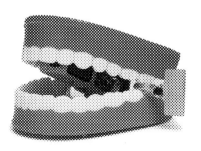

PERSPECTIVE PRACTICE 2: BE TRUE TO YOURSELF

The hamster-wheel of life is designed to trap you. The purpose of our short time on earth should be to really engage in what it is to be human. To do that properly we have to both engage in and enjoy the human struggle. We therefore have very little concept of anything else but this human reality. We only focus upon what's in front of us, the pressures of work, the commute, what we will do at the weekend, how we will make enough money, the difficulties of bringing up a family, our expanding bellies and receding hairlines, the state of the economy, our looming review day, the last series of *24*, saving for our retirement, paying off the mortgage, the next promotion, and all that jazz. None of that is really important, though. When we die, none of it will matter one jot. The dilemma we have is how to have a full, rich, human experience – which inevitably involves those pressures and worries and angst – while still remembering that it's all one big game and that none of it really matters in the end.

Energetically we exist on a spectrum. At one end of the spectrum is our normal life, where we focus on our daily activities. At the other end of the spectrum we are – as Carl Jung would say – part of the 'collective consciousness', and here we lose our personal identity and can access all the resources available to humankind.

To really make the most of this life we need to develop the skill to move along that spectrum at will. We need to be grounded and useful, while still connecting to the essence of who we are.

Next time you feel isolated, stuck, power-less, or frustrated by the small things, stop.

None of those sensations are real. They are just a perspective. Sit straight, breathe, smile, feel your body falling back, and connect to who you really are.

This takes some practice, but remember that we all connect with our energetic selves regularly. Some do so deliberately through meditation, exercise, family, sleep; others do so when they are struck by a sunset or make a connection with a friend. It happens all the time but is most useful if you can do it every day, by choice. Then you will have a perspective that will be bulletproof – one that no ill-judged action or business hardship can dent. The small things will never matter unless you decide they should, and that's a wonderful place to work from.

All you have to do is breathe, sit straight, smile. With practice you will feel different, with the energy coursing around your body.

Don't concentrate too much, just smile and let go of all the stuff that is no longer important.

Do this as often as you can, and you'll soon be able to zoom between the two.

You'll never be stuck.

LIVE IT, DON'T THINK IT

It's all too tempting to spend our lives thinking too much, worrying about the future or wishing things could be better.

When it comes to doing new and different things our rational brain more often hinders our movement than helps. Its ability to incapacitate is legendary. It can spiral into a doom-laden scenario with the smallest piece of data.

Instead of imagining it, live it. Do something real and try something out.

The experience is often surprising. Most people find that when they try things out, the reality is so different from what they imagined that it is refreshing and freeing. So if you have plans that seem to have faltered, just carry them out anyway. See what happens and learn. At least then you will have perfect data, real feedback. Whether your plan succeeds or fails, you will at least know.

I once arranged a first-aid course for my team. They are all top-flight facilitators and must be rather intimidating to train as they spend their lives developing the best talent around the world. The trainer we had was unflustered and taught us not only how to save lives, but to have more impact.

He must have been in his late fifties and was old school in style. His opener was to draw a ship hitting an iceberg on the flipchart. He then asked what it was. Someone said the Titanic, to which he replied, 'Yes, breaks the ice, doesn't it?' We were struck by his cheesy confidence and bad gags; he started to win us over.

On day two, after explaining how to deal with choking, he asked one of the team to turn on his mobile phone and be ready to call the emergency services in case his demonstration went wrong. He then dipped a tissue into some water and inhaled it, so it became stuck in his throat and made him choke.

He started to turn red, eyes bulging. Stunned, it took me a second or two to register what was happening. I then jumped into action, doing what he'd just explained that we should.

I slapped him once on the back. Nothing. Next time was harder. Still nothing. I reasoned that he was a big guy, so could take the force of a third and harder slap, and frankly I wasn't keen on moving to a Heimlich manoeuvre. It worked fabulously and dislodged the tissue. He gasped fresh air once more.

My guess is that he was in control all the way through and his performance was nothing more than great theatre. However, the way I reacted was real – the surge of adrenaline, the feedback that I wasn't hitting him hard enough. What I will never forget is the power needed to dislodge a tissue from a large man's throat. It was real and I had learned it for ever.

It also set up his next gag perfectly when he asked for a volunteer. He was carrying a tin of paraffin and a Zippo and announced it was now time to learn how to treat burns. Classic, old school; deeply memorable.

Get stuck in

Next time you find yourself sitting in a meeting debating the pros and cons of different plans and trying to predict the future, remember that you have two choices.

You can carry on this intellectual arm-wrestling contest until every avenue has been explored and all in the room are beautifully aligned in their divination of what the forthcoming years will hold. Alternatively, you can just get stuck in and try things out and know that the feedback you get from those experiments is real. You can adapt those approaches depending upon what you learn.

Many companies avoid experimentation because they believe there's a risk to their brand. That is fear-induced rubbish. What they are really scared of is getting things wrong and how that would look.

If your brand is so weak that some innovative experimentation will damage it for good, you'd better spend more time on your brand. If the truth is that you hate getting things wrong, you'd better wake up to the twenty-first century, where things happen so fast you don't have a chance to polish the idea, to test things perfectly, to guarantee that every segment of every demographic is happy with your offer. You need to do it now or you'll be lost.

If you are clever enough you can always find a reason why things won't work. If, instead, you just do it, you can always find ways to make it better.

Go and get your hands dirty; don't just talk about it, do it.

BUY LESS CRAP

We are devoted to accumulating crap. The media is constantly telling us we need new stuff, better stuff, shinier stuff. When we go looking for that stuff and finally buy it, it satisfies a primal urge akin to that of a kill by a hunter. But just like the kill, the purchase is only briefly satisfying – it can only fill a hole temporarily. We are then driven to buy more.

Many business executives never enjoy what they have because they are forever focusing on what's next, what's bigger, what's brighter. They become trapped in jobs that can never deliver the lifestyle they want.

When people go to work in finance, they often say, 'I'll do it for ten years, bank a couple of million, and then do something I truly love.' Thirty years later when they have made tens of millions they are still flogging their guts out in the City. They've been caught on the lifestyle escalator and don't know how to get off.

Don't become trapped by the same fate. Appreciate what a wonderful life you have. Know that buying more crap won't make you happy and that the richer people in the world worry about how to manage all those houses and yachts just as you worry about the weekly shop or saving for your holidays.

Next time you are tempted to buy something that you don't truly need, stop and think.

If you decide that you really need to buy crap, buy the best crap available. Get something that is exceptional, something that costs a lot and in which you can take great pleasure for years to come. At least the crap you own will have class and durability. And if you buy the best there is, you can't be tempted by something better.

And after you've bought it, solemnly swear not to buy any more crap for at least a month.

GET FRESH

Our brains always draw on our past experiences for inspiration and simple solutions. It's a fast and natural way to make sure our learning is applied and that we act efficiently. Although efficiency is great for making things happen, it's the opposite of creativity. Being efficient usually means doing something the way that we have always done it, often without thinking. We get the job done, but we also become well and truly stuck.

To get fresh, you have to break habits and do things differently. This will keep your brain stimulated and will help you find flexible perspectives.

I once persuaded 30,000 people to break their habits for five days, starting with simple things like sleeping on the other side of the bed or swapping their iPod with a friend's. More habits were added as the week progressed.

By the end of the experiment I had received mountains of positive feedback about the way people felt – freer, with better ideas and more energy.

I love the novel *The Dice Man* by Luke Rhinehart, where the lead character lets the roll of a dice decide his fate. It forces freshness into his life. To leave every decision to chance means things will never be dull.

Apple founder Steve Jobs created freshness in his life when he dropped out of college. He still attended classes, but only the ones that he was interested in. One of those classes was calligraphy. Steve was interested in it but had no reason to believe that it would be of any particular benefit to his life.

Years later when he was designing the Mac, it all came back to him. That's why the Mac had such beautiful typography and a new way of laying out symbols. This became the benchmark for every computer in the world.

Freshness is a strategic choice; it's not an investment that pays back in a linear way. It is surprising. It cannot guarantee a breakthrough idea, but it can guarantee a much greater chance of having one. Most importantly, it can guarantee that your journey through life will be much richer.

Mess with everything: it keeps your brain fresh and your creativity pumping. Life will never be dull.

TAKE A LOOK AT YOUR HABITS INSIDE AND OUTSIDE WORK

Most of them aren't even conscious.

If you always get a coffee first thing, go somewhere else and try a smoothie.

If you have a regular meeting each month, change the day, venue, timing, people.

If you have to conduct reviews and always do them at end of year, shake it up and do it half-yearly or quarterly. This will give you more chance to influence people's brilliance.

Take different routes to work, move your desk, take up a lunchtime hobby, hang out with the guys from Finance, dress differently.

Imagine you have just been sacked: now what would you do?

Go home for lunch and surprise whoever is there. Could be surprising for you too!

BEWARE ANAESTHETICS

When you drive hard in business, you become less aware of how you are faring.

We've all had days when we've forgotten to have lunch even though our bodies were craving nutrition. When you work so fast it's easy to lose touch, not only with your body but with your feelings and your sensitivity to the world around you.

One way we manage to maintain this speed is to numb ourselves with anaesthetics. Some of them are obvious: alcohol, nicotine, drugs. But others are more subtle: coffee, TV, iPods, crazy diary appointments, overeating, energy drinks, shopping, social networking, gaming. All these can act as anaesthetics because potentially they deaden the experience of being human, by either desensitizing us or protecting us from the stimulus of the outside world.

To shine you need to be connected to your responses and how your body feels. You need to notice what's changing in the world around you (and, most importantly, the people in it). If you are turbo-driven with only the end goal in sight, it's hard to react to those changes and make the most of opportunities as they arise.

Walk through any city on a weekday morning and you will find people clutching huge takeaway coffees, drinking through a tiny hole in the lid and feeling warm inside. Never have I seen a more effective comfort blanket; this particular anaesthetic makes work feel better.

If work feels that bad, don't numb yourself or distract yourself from the real issue. Make work fantastic and devote every minute of your day to making sure it's the same for others.

You need to be aware of the world in all its glory, so you can make better decisions. Numb is robotic, half dead. Wake up and feel it.

PAIN AND PLEASURE

The secret to getting anything done lies in the classic pain and pleasure equation. If you associate pain with carrying on as you are, then you will have an incentive to do things differently. If, however, carrying on as you are produces no pain, nothing will change.

Much of my time is spent helping big businesses innovate better. My clients all agree that it's a fantastic thing to do – who wouldn't? I've never had any senior execs who would publicly say that innovation wasn't important.

But the reality of making it happen is different. Those execs have built their careers on a set of skills that have become habitual. The prospect of doing things differently can be frightening; self-identity is at stake.

To help them overcome their fear and live innovation on a daily basis, I tweak their pain and pleasure equation. I make sure that they are aware of it every single day. I do that by helping them paint horrific pictures of the future created by a business-as-usual approach. They must really feel the torment of that dystopia from every possible perspective. This is not an intellectual exercise; it has to be visceral.

I balance the equation by painting a picture of the pleasure to be gained by embracing a culture of innovation. The energy created in such a process must then be revisited every day to ensure that the commitment to change becomes part of their DNA.

To be Elvis in your business, you need to get things done.

Procrastination is a waste of energy. Either decide to abandon the project or get on and do it, and do it with all your heart. Be sure that all your energy is working for you by manipulating your own pain and pleasure equation in such a way that you have no choice. It then becomes no longer a question of if ... just how and when.

DON'T HAVE ALL THE ANSWERS

One of my client companies has a 'just in case' culture. What that means is that there are people staying in the office till 10 p.m. or even midnight preparing PowerPoint presentations, 'just in case' they are asked a particular tricky question.

This creates the most toxic of conditions in business. The message that goes out is that if somebody senior asks a question and you don't know the answer, you are in deep trouble. This drives a culture of fear and supports the premise that one person can have all the answers.

This is crazy. The world is so dynamic that even trying to have one per cent of the answers in your head would make your brain explode. The idea of being so smart that you can know everything and predict the future is pure fantasy.

Every business needs a group of leaders who can deal with ambiguity, change and surprises. The nature of the business environment means you can never have all the answers; the best leaders are the ones who are resourceful and creative enough to know where to find them when necessary.

The idea of leaders being geniuses is actually destructive – and the impact filters through to all employees, who start believing that to be a leader you have to have all the answers (an impossible goal). It also means that nobody is prepared to share a half-formed thought that might fuel new ideas. Two heads are always better than one, so imagine how good linking together the brainpower of a whole organization must be. Whenever someone is too scared to share their thinking early, a potentially extraordinary breakthrough is stillborn.

So, be confident that you can't always know the answers, and don't expect your people to. It's simply unreasonable.

Don't be afraid to say you are unsure. Share your worries and concerns about predicting the future. Be honest when you are lost and ask for help; doing so will encourage a more honest conversation with the whole business.

You will be saying, 'What we value are people who are curious, intuitive and smart.' People who can find out their own answers and make sense of this beautiful world.

PERSPECTIVE PRACTICE 3: QUESTION YOUR ASSUMPTIONS

Our impressions of who we are and where we add value are built up over many years. Every experience we have could influence our map of the world; the more emotionally resonant, the more profound the impact.

If an aeroplane alters its course by just one degree at the beginning of its journey from Hong Kong to Brussels, it could end up over Holland and miss Belgium altogether. (Quelle désastre; no moules et frites!)

We have a similar problem. Our early beliefs shape who we are. They affect how we filter information and are key to all our decisions. Before long they have moulded who we are, how we perceive and where we are going. For example, if a concerned mother keeps stressing to her child that the world is full of bad people, the child soon starts to believe it. That belief is then reinforced by paying selective attention to the evil in this world and ignoring the good in it.

This is exactly what the world's media do every day. That's why so many people live in fear. We have to break away from that cycle of reinforcement to be really alive.

Planes don't fly in straight lines and neither do we. But pilots adjust their flight path constantly, ensuring that they remain on course to reach their intended destination. We, however, set a course and then allow life's dynamism to blow us around willy-nilly, using only our warped perspectives to keep us on track. By becoming flexible in our perceptions we have more chance of not heading off in the wrong direction.

To become flexible we need to constantly question our assumptions. We need to fill our lives with new stimuli that challenge our perceptions of who we are and what is important.

WHO ARE YOU AND WHAT DO YOU WANT?

IT MAY SOUND SIMPLE, BUT THESE ARE QUESTIONS THAT REALLY COUNT. USUALLY YOUR FIRST ANSWER IS NOT TRUE.

SIT, BREATHE, SMILE AND ASK THE QUESTION AGAIN. GO A LITTLE **DEEPER.**

SURROUND YOURSELF WITH INTERESTING PEOPLE

I never understand how people can be bored. This planet has so much going on, it's like Disneyland every day.

One constant source of stimulation and inspiration is people. Everyone has something to share, something of value; we just need to find it.

We can now connect with people easily through a clutch of internet networking sites: LinkedIn, Facebook, FourSquare, etc. If you make a list of your fantasy business mates, chances are you can connect with them – at least electronically.

There are those who shine just a little more brightly, and have something a little more compelling about who they are and what they say.

Make them a part of your life and two things will happen. First, your life will never be dull, but rich with ideas and unusual perspectives. Second, you will become more interesting yourself.

USING YOUR POSITION
TO CONTROL OTHERS

Using hierarchical power is the last resort of those who have run out of options or time.

I was briefly in the army, where there is little time to do much else other than shout or follow orders. It gets the job done, but this is no way to win hearts and minds in the business world. Weak leaders do it because it's easy and quick and takes no talent, but it is almost always counter-productive.

Don't do it.

THREE CHOICES

Whenever you find yourself in a situation that isn't that great for you, you have three choices: avoid, accept or adapt.

There are some circumstances in life where it's just easier to avoid the person or the situation that isn't filling you with great energy. This is not a cop-out, it's a conscious decision to avoid something that is too difficult or painful to change and you can't possibly accept it. The best tactic is to then excise it from your life as far as possible.

The second option is acceptance. It takes real wisdom to understand when the situation is best accepted, but if you can truly accept what you can't change, it can be a liberating experience. To accept something that you have previously been reluctant to embrace will require some changes in your perspective. When you do so, however, your energy can be saved for the more important battles with those things you can neither avoid nor accept but must adapt.

Adapting is the most difficult and energy-draining

option. In this context it means not changing your attitude but altering the situation so that you can interact positively with it. Changing the world is always exhausting, so only choose to adapt when you have no other option and you are confident of success.

Next time there is somebody or something bothering you, ponder which of the three options will give you what you want for the minimum outlay of energy. If you use the right combination on your to-do list today, you will find that annoyances and energy-sappers are easily dealt with.

WHEN WE ARE DOING SOMETHING THAT WE **ENJOY** IT IS MUCH EASIER TO BE SHINY, AND **TIME JUST** FLIES BY.

IF IT AIN'T FUN, STOP DOING IT

We spend on average forty hours a week at work, another ten or more commuting to and from it, and much of our evenings and weekends thinking about it. We probably even spend some of our time asleep dreaming about it. Work is a huge part of who we are and how we self-express.

If we don't enjoy it, a vast proportion of our life is being wasted.

We owe it to ourselves to make sure that the work that we do – though it might not touch our very soul – can at least be fun. When we are doing something that we enjoy it is much easier to be shiny, and time just flies by. When we're hating it, that's torture.

I find ways to make things amusing. On a recent contract negotiation (save me, please!), I decided to be as nice and as generous as I could; this is the opposite of traditional business wisdom. The contract was with one of the world's largest businesses and the previous negotiations had taken nine painful months.

(By the end of them the relationship was strained, as was my sanity.)

This time, with my new approach, the whole thing was wrapped up within two days after about ten minutes of chat. I was given a better deal than ever before and we all felt fantastic about our partnership.

Next time, my objective will be to seduce the lawyer … A step too far? We'll see. But certainly more fun.

ONE BIG THING

Every morning when you arrive at work, identify the One Big Thing that you need to achieve before you go home.

So often I see people sit down at their desk, turn on their computer and start reacting to the world and what the world wants. Many of them won't take their eyes from their screens until it's time to leave. They have spent the entire day out of control, working to other people's agendas. What is your agenda?

If you are clear on where you are going, you can be clear on what you have to do each day – the One Big Thing.

This then becomes your focus, which means you have a very high chance of achieving it. At the end of the day you'll know whether it's been a good one or not and can adapt your approach accordingly.

We love being distracted; we love to multi-task and to play with all our toys in our sandboxes; busy feels important and effective. But it also dilutes our energy. It's impossible to have impact when your attention is divided among so many projects, conversations, and pleas for help.

When you're working with your team, every time you have any interaction with them, ask them what their One Big Thing is today.

If they can't answer that, then you need to coach them until they can. At the end of the day when they say goodnight you can then ask whether they have achieved the Big Thing or not. You then can reward and congratulate or make a note to help them out next day. Without this focus your people's development and achievement will lose edge and power. And the same applies to you.

A friend of mine, Shilen, told me about a really interesting guy he'd met in a Las Vegas casino. He was betting big and obviously loving every minute. They got into conversation and it emerged that the high roller had made his money in publishing. Shilen was intrigued, as self-made millionaires are a scarce commodity; especially in publishing.

The manner in which the man had made his cash was incredibly single-minded, not to mention a little bizarre. First, he'd written an algorithm that identified the most common search term on the internet that elicited the least information. The answer was 'parrots'.

He then went to a well-known zoo, found the parrot expert there and commissioned him to write a book on parrots. He published the first chapter free online and then made the rest of it downloadable for a fee. The results were astonishing.

In the first month he made hundreds of thousands of dollars; in the first year millions. Being in his early twenties and living in India, you can see why the tables in Vegas had a certain allure for him.

Parrot Man had One Big Thing and he went for it with all his energy. The purity of his idea and his single-minded focus has brought him huge rewards.

If you always know what your One Big Thing is, you have a much greater chance of success.

BE A DICK, NOT A COCK

I know that this heading might sound a bit ridiculous but it ended up guiding my entire recruitment strategy incredibly successfully for many years. I have to thank my friend and ex-colleague Simon Bray for introducing me to the concept (although his original language was somewhat spicier).

In this context, a dick is an endearing name for somebody who self-expresses in a playful and creative fashion and sometimes gets it wrong. The beauty of it is that they don't care when they make a fool of themselves, because they know that life is about experimentation and having a laugh. These are the people I like to surround myself with. They are the risk takers, the ones who will try new things and are constantly challenging me. The fact that I am writing about this in a business book, published by Penguin, makes me a bit of a dick. If you are reading this, I guess my editor values them too. A cock, however, is not somebody you want to be around. Never confuse the two.

<u>COMMIT</u>

So many people in business waste their time because of a lack of commitment.

'My job is OK, but I don't truly love it.' 'This project could be big, but the board could sack it tomorrow.'

There is something within them that sabotages their energy. If you constantly question who you are and the impact that you have, you will never be as shiny as you could be.

At some point you have to jump in with both feet. Say to yourself, 'All right, this may not be perfect but today I'll give it all I am.' By doing so your energy will have a hundred times more impact and your satisfaction levels will skyrocket.

Business has too many spectators, too many critics, and the cynicism is rampant. If people don't like their work they should either change the way they do it or leave. Are you committed to being as good as you can possibly be in your role? If not, how can you change things so that you become committed? If you can't think of anything, then polish up that CV. It's either all-in or all-out.

TRAVEL

I remember being with a friend of mine the first time he saw the sea. It was extraordinary. No one can imagine truly what the ocean is like until they have taken off their shoes and waded in, jumping the waves, smelling the salt and feeling the swell.

There is a whole planet out there waiting to be explored. The diversity of nature, people and cultures is what can make this adventure resonant. The difference between even the north and south of Italy is profound, let alone Iowa versus Karachi.

Travel keeps you fresh, tolerant and always open to new experiences. Get a ticket, get a buzz.

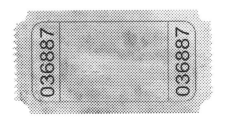

HANG OUT WITH RESONATORS, NOT VAMPIRES

Some people can walk into a disastrous situation and still turn it into a party. Other people seem to take the most exquisite enjoyable celebration and turn it into hell.

The first group I would call resonators. These people have an energy that is infectious. They believe anything is possible and they believe that everything should be fun.

My friend Andy and I were flying back from Shanghai when we were delayed by snow, missed our connecting flights and were stranded in Hong Kong airport with jet lag, exhaustion from running workshops and hangovers from Moutai. Andy managed to turn the occasion into an adventure, a game, and an all-round enriching experience. The time flew by and new friends were made in the process.

I want Andy and other resonators like him to be around me all the time.

Resonators pop up in all sorts of places and in all sorts of shapes and sizes. They possess a force that is hard to describe and impossible to resist.

I have spent many years trying to change people into resonators and I'm afraid to say I have failed. You can't build them from scratch, you can only up their power. However, we can surround ourselves with them so we have the support to do new things.

Who knows, by osmosis you too could transform into a master resonator. If you are already one: bravo.

Vampires, on the other hand, love taking energy away; they love the drama they create, the difficulty that spews out from every action that they take. They may explain how they hate being like that but the truth is they get some kind of payback, otherwise they'd just whistle a happy tune instead.

I have tried to encourage those I've met to become energy givers, but I've reached the conclusion that it's better to avoid them. They are intractable, yet strangely amusing, forever caught in the most desperate of dramas. If they are in your team, sack them. If they are 'friends', sack them. If you are married to one ... take up drinking.

DO ICONIC

If your resources are limited and you are in an environment where everyone is clamouring for attention, just do the big stuff.

Find a project that's significant, so that when you nail it everyone will be talking about it. Aim to do something that will become the stuff of legend, a project that can be your legacy. When you come across such an opportunity, throw everything you have at it to guarantee its sparkly success.

By doing so your profile will be super-enhanced, to a far greater degree than if you were to expend the same effort over ten averagely interesting projects.

Once, at dinner with some friends, I met a lovely guy who I can only think of as Bramble Man. He had invented the fantastic cocktail that is the Bramble. He lives for ever in my mind as the legend responsible for one of my favourite drinks. God bless the Bramble.

I recently saw a YouTube clip that explained how an American called Alec Brownstein used Google AdWords to get the attention of the creative directors he wanted to work for. When they Googled their names, as all creative directors should, an ad with his name on it popped up saying, 'Googling yourself is a lot of fun. Hiring me is fun too.'

It cost him six dollars. He was offered two jobs and is now a senior copywriter at the Young & Republican advertising agency in New York. Simple, iconic action that made young Alec stand out from the crowd.

And that's what doing iconic projects is all about; making a lasting impression that creates a halo around you.

CHILL AND LAUGH

People who are overly serious are doomed in two ways.

First, they will have a miserable life and die young, regretting those moments when they could have run barefoot in the grass, tipsy on champagne, wearing a pixie hat.

Second, those poor people only get to use a fraction of their brain. Supposedly 'clever' serious people get stuck in their conscious-processing jail (which neuroscience tells us could be as little as 4 per cent of our potential genius). If only they would relax and have some fun they would tap much more of their potential. When you relax you access the massive processor and storage unit that is your subconscious.

So the next time you find yourself stuck, laugh and daydream. Make some faces. Dance around the office on the way to your favourite person on that floor. Watch some comedy DVDs or anything that makes you chuckle; the type of laugh where your whole belly moves and you can't breathe.

Think of what puts you in that happy place and recreate wherever and whenever you need it. I put on some Josh Rouse tunes and my Lycra pants and all is good in the world.

You have the choice: be stuck in serious, or lark about and be very smart indeed.

Simple, eh?

MAKE FRIENDS AND DUMP SOME

Gone are the days when an individual or even an organization had all the skills and know-how to be exceptional in everything. We all need help from specialists, those who have developed so well in a particular field that it makes no sense for us to develop ourselves.

If you have been hanging out with interesting people, you no doubt already know some of them. They have the ability to transform what you do and connect you with others who can explode your thinking. Having friends in interesting places means you are never short of options and can always find help when it's needed.

To make space for these new buddies, get rid of some old ones. As the years roll on we change and develop. We need to spring clean our lives, and especially those to whom we devote our precious time. Friends take investment, so dump the ones you feel no longer fit, and give your new ones the energy they need.

Sounds harsh, but it is better to do it consciously than to just drift away and be known as flaky.

WEAR CLOTHES THAT UP YOUR ENERGY, PHYSICALLY AND MENTALLY. WEAR CLOTHES THAT REPRESENT WHO YOU ARE TO THE WORLD WHILE STILL MAKING YOU FEEL GREAT.

YOU WEAR IT WELL

There is far too much talk about 'business dress'. Having your colours done, power dressing and being styled are all much-publicized pursuits of the thrusting executive.

It's not that I'm against those activities, but I do think they're adding more snake oil to the mix than is necessary.

For you to shine brightly, you need to feel good. We all have clothes that make us feel trussed up and restricted and we have others that make us feel relaxed, invincible or even irresistible. Choose the latter and you will find it a lot easier to be yourself.

The pressure in business is to conform in the way we speak, the way we think and the way we dress. If doing so makes you feel as if you're not being your true self, stop it.

Wear clothes that up your energy, physically and mentally. Wear clothes that represent who you are to the world while still making you feel great.

If there is anything in your wardrobe that doesn't do

that, pack it up and ship it off to a charity that really needs them. Dressing in the morning is much easier when you know full well that everything that you have is right for you. And that is where a good stylist can be useful, clearing away the crap.

Only wear clothes that you can really carry off. If you can't walk beautifully in high heels and don't love the way they feel, don't wear them. If a tie makes you feel as if your head is not connected to your body, don't wear one. If the casual uniform of modern-day business is chinos and a polo shirt and you hate that look, wear something else.

I remember speaking to the top seventy execs at Ritz Carlton. It was an impressive gathering, and because these guys were in the high-end hospitality game, they were all impeccably attired. Their suits were cut to perfection and they wore them well.

I was told that I needed to suit up too, otherwise my message might be less well received. I will never forget it. I hate suits. I chose one that was rather funky, but it still wasn't me. I felt disconnected from myself and therefore was not on my usual energetic and infectious form. I was flat and stilted.

Since that day I have always dressed only for me, and it feels good. If people don't like how I look then the chances are we won't get on anyway, so it just speeds up the selection process.

Amass a wardrobe you like, discard anything that doesn't make you feel good, and never ever dress for anyone else (unless it's in a saucy weekend stylie).

REALLY FEELY

Intuition can be explained in many ways. Whether it's your subconscious letting you know that it has seen something interesting, or whether you're tapping into the universal consciousness, intuition is a fantastic ally to have.

Intuition is a priceless asset. Often we can't work out what to do using our tiny conscious brains. It's too confusing and there are far too many variables to predict the right path. That's when you want intuition on your side.

To get it working for you, program your intuition to know what it is looking for. The way to do this is to make an imagined situation real. Your intuition doesn't work on a conceptual basis; it only responds to the absolute. So you have to experience your options to get it to work most efficiently.

For example, if you are stuck and can't decide on the best course of action, just pick one at random. You don't have to act upon it yet, just decide that that is what you will do. Then live with that decision and visualize yourself carrying it through.

Notice your reactions to that future. Notice what goes on in your body and in your mind, particularly how it affects your sense of connection to yourself, your colleagues and your business. Some decisions feel fantastic as soon as you make them and you know they are right in every cell of your body; others feel utterly wrong, giving you clear and simple direction.

If you're still unconvinced that your decision was correct then rescind it, make a different one and repeat the process. If you find difficulty in making it real, tell a few people what your decision is going to be and that will reinforce the reality for you. Again notice how you feel as you live with that decision.

'Trying on' different options allows your intuition to react, giving you a better idea of how they might turn out, and how they fit with your needs and desires. Your intuition can only let you know by changing the way you feel, so you have to be sensitive to what it tells you.

If a project has three routes that look exciting and you can't decide which one to take, pursue all three for a week each. Notice which of them feels the most fertile.

The best innovators I know in business are highly intuitive. They can't tell you why they've made decisions, they just know that one option feels better than the other and are confident enough to trust their feelings over muddled logic.

We are designed to have instincts, we are designed to feel our way through life, so if you can tap into that you will find that life flows.

Get out of your head, make it real and then feel your way.

FEEDBACK WITH FUNK

The word 'feedback' often has terrible connotations. When someone tells you that they have some feedback for you, more often than not you are filled with dread: generally it means you've done something wrong.

It is also used as a tool to make us do what others want us to. So our growth and development is often muddied with managerial agenda.

Feedback is how we learn in life. We try something out and we notice what happens and then adjust what we do next accordingly.

One problem is that we tend to have quite a warped perception of ourselves, our performance and the impact we have; to shine brightly we need to crave feedback on a daily basis and continually ask others how we are doing. By doing so we will constantly improve both our game and our awareness of who we are, what we do and the impact of our actions.

One of the reasons feedback has such a bad reputation is that it is often badly delivered. Another reason is that feedback seems to be offered mainly when things have gone wrong. If you really want to help somebody learn and grow they have to know what they are doing brilliantly as well as the things that need some work.

My rule of thumb – inspired by one of Malcolm Gladwell's books – is that for every one piece of developmental feedback (i.e. on something that could be done better), I offer five pieces of reinforcing feedback (i.e. on things that are being done fantastically).

That way, the person I am giving feedback to is in no doubt that I am on their side, and therefore they can take on the learning more easily.

I seek out feedback every day – which isn't that difficult as I am on stage, speaking to groups, working with teams and running large events. Over the years I have received a lot of it. Some of the most useless examples are: 'Chris, that was fantastic!' 'Chris, loved your energy!' 'Chris, think you were a bit off message on that.'

All these comments are non-specific. What exactly was fantastic? What was it about my energy that you loved, and how did that show up? What precisely was off message?

Without detail, feedback is useless. Being told I'm

simply 'fantastic' gives me no clue about what I should do more of the next time. Being told that the way I manage the interaction of the groups in a humorous way means that people let down their guard lets me know that I could use that approach again.

Another problem is that the context in which feedback is given can often be confused. Feedback should be offered as an aid to learning how to develop you. You should then be able to choose how you react to that feedback; you should not be forced to change what you do based upon it.

A key to giving great feedback is the spirit in which it is offered. The intention must be to help the person receiving it grow.

Here's a feedback process that I have found invaluable in my development and in changing the cultures of many businesses.

Stage One: Check-in

Before sharing any feedback you have to
make sure that you are in the right place
to give it and they are in the right place
to receive it. Ask yourself: are you in the
right state and do you have good intention?
Never give feedback when you are cross or
frustrated with someone because you are then
attached to what they do with it. That isn't
funky feedback. That's manipulative mischief.

Also, people aren't always in the right state to
take on new learning. They may be distracted,
tired or angry, so your pearls of wisdom will
be wasted. If that is the case, arrange a time
that is good for both of you.

Stage Two: Data

All feedback needs to be based on precise events or activity. Something that has happened which both parties can agree upon.

For example: 'In a meeting yesterday with our client from Coca-Cola we overran by one hour. It was my anniversary and I was worried I would be late for dinner with my wife. We had a taxi waiting and you said I could take the taxi straight home, while you would take the bus.'

Those are the facts. At this point whoever you're giving feedback to needs to agree that that's what happened. If you cannot agree on the events, giving feedback becomes a tricky thing indeed, so make sure you can identify exactly what happened. Give feedback as soon after the event as possible to aid clarity.

Stage Three: Interpretation

You then share how you interpreted that data or event.

'That made me think that you're really good at understanding what is most important in people's lives, and prioritizing the person over the business or yourself.'

This interpretation is yours; therefore it cannot be wrong.

Stage Four: Reaction

You then share how you feel as a result of that event and your interpretation of it.

'So on the way home in the car I felt fantastic because I was going to make sure that the important person in my life had a wonderful evening. Because you put me above yourself in that situation I want to do the same for you in the future … and I like working for a business where people's lives are as important as profit.'

Stage Five: Land it

Your colleague now gets a chance to land it any way that they want.

They might say: 'Actually, I preferred to take the bus home as I wanted to do some shopping and I couldn't do that if we shared a cab.'

Or it may be something more like this: 'Hey, that's really useful. It was a bit of a hassle taking the bus, but I could see you were getting nervous.'

With this feedback technique it's very easy to make sense of what the feedback is and what you can do as a result of it.

Although the steps may feel a little clunky, with time and practice the process becomes more fluid. The key to its success is twofold.

First, make sure you have a good intention. Do not use this technique to vent grievances, manipulate colleagues or just plain have a go. If you do, it's ruined.

Second, make sure that you separate the data from the interpretation. As long as you do those two things, it will work.

This technique is used by many organizations and goes by many different names, such as data-based feedback technique, good intentioned feedback technique, or truth speaking. I call it funky feedback, but you can call it Bernard.

Top tip: If you want to give somebody feedback, do not start by saying: 'Hey, I've got some feedback for you.' More than likely, this will send them into a spiral of gloom. Instead try: 'Hey, I spotted something that I think might be useful for you, would you like to hear about it?'

Use feedback well and it will reward you beyond riches.

KICK BACK, GAZE OUT OF THE WINDOW AND ENJOY.

DAYDREAM

All those teachers who told you to stop daydreaming in class were wrong.

Daydreaming is great for us.

It's a way of de-stressing and letting our brains deal with all the learning and stimulus that comes into our little heads. Without some processing time, it is easy to feel overwhelmed.

Daydreaming is also a great way of connecting with our subconscious in order to have new ideas. When we let our minds wander we often come back with an insight or idea that helps us move forward.

So kick back, gaze out of the window and enjoy.

Big tip: Write down whatever it was you were thinking about when 'outside that window'. It could be pure genius.

GANG OF THREE

Since the invention of the wheel, many captains of industry have stood alone at the summit of their empires.

That's a difficult position to occupy, and most people who do so are lonely and isolated. Many of them search for support outside their organization because it is hard for a boss to get real support and worthwhile opinion from those lower down. It's an even trickier place to be if you adopt the traditional leadership style of having to have the answers, make the decisions and be an all-round superhero.

Life becomes a little easier if the burden is shared. Collaborative two-way partnerships have been incredibly successful, especially in creative pursuits, and are still a core part of what's left of the traditional advertising industry today. Two people can form a deep bond, and a partner can often bring different skills and perspectives to the work.

I know from personal experience how useful such partnerships can be. But they are far from perfect.

Like nearly all relationships, a partnership has a shelf life. Very few last the test of time while still producing world-class output. And, by God, partners so often bicker.

But there is a better way. In business, the magic number is three. Having three people who are tight enough to lead a team, department or business has all the benefits and none of the downsides of one- or two-person leadership.

In a triumvirate, no one can relax. No one can become complacent or comfortable with their position because if they do the other two will run ahead. It's important that the three members are diverse, because there will then always be somebody to work with who has a different perspective.

In my view, the gang of three is more effective and better than the other options. (The gang of four becomes two partnerships quite quickly; I also know from experience that it's lonely being on your own.)

Having been in a gang of three, and seen many others up close, I believe it has real advantages. Its members don't all have to be equal. The important thing is that they're aligned and devoted to a singular vision, and will support each other in making that vision real. It doesn't even have to be a formalized relationship, but when it works it is something that the whole team would die on a sword for.

And if anyone advises you that a three-way split is a bad idea, just tell them it worked for God.

THOUGHTS DON'T CHANGE THE WORLD – IDEAS DO

Many of the frustrations that business experiences concerning brainstorming, creativity and innovation are rooted in a failure to appreciate the difference between a thought and an idea, or indeed the value of that difference.

Thoughts are very useful as stepping stones to an idea, but no one ever made money from a thought. Ideas, on the other hand, could potentially be of enormous value.

For example, 'We need to sort out our supply chain' is a thought, but it offers no idea of what the revised supply chain will look like or how it will be achieved. An idea from that starting thought could be, 'Next Tuesday in our meeting with the head of supply, let's share our concerns about the supply chain's deficiencies and put forward three suggestions to improve things. One of those suggestions will be a "cynic clinic", so we can find out what's on everyone's minds.'

Now that's something that we can do.

Thoughts are dust in the wind.

Ideas are gold in our pockets.

Idea Wizardry

It's really important that your ideas are captured in the right way.

At Upping Your Elvis we know we have done something right when it passes the 'Envelope Test'. The test comprises one simple question: 'If I were to put the idea in an envelope and send it to Jo Foster, innovator extraordinaire, would she be able to do the idea?' If the idea has been captured with sufficient detail and clarity then Jo will be able to see it instantly.

If the essence of the idea isn't delivered, Jo won't be able to do a thing with it.

In which case it's a waste of everyone's time.

WHAT DO THEY WANT FROM YOU?

There are broadly two ways to think in business.

The first, largely overdeveloped, style of thinking is analytical, logical and reductionist. This type of processing takes place almost entirely in our conscious brain and therefore has limited power.

The second is one that we all have a natural ability to do but all too rarely practise: creative and expansive thinking.

Both of these thinking styles are absolutely crucial to the success of anyone in business. Most of our working day will be spent using good logical thinking, but at times logic isn't enough and we must switch the dial to the 'creative master' setting.

Knowing when to switch can be a challenge. It's important that we realize exactly what our objectives are at any given time because what helps us get into a logical state can be quite different from what gets us into a creative one. So when you are doing a piece of work, ask yourself, 'What do I need now?' Would commercial, analytical thinking or creative, insightful, expansive thinking be better?

This becomes even more important when you're working with other people. I am sure you have been in a meeting when somebody has said, 'I've got this great idea …', and someone else has responded with, 'We've tried that already and it was too expensive.' What you are seeing are two people in different thinking modes: the creative ('This idea might increase profit in the long term') and the logical ('This idea will reduce profit in the short term and is not guaranteed to succeed, so why take the risk?'), which usually ends in a dust-up.

If you really want to shine in business, every time you have an interaction with somebody, ask what they want from you. Do they want you to be commercial, logical and analytical, or do they want you to help them be creative and build on their idea?

This sounds simple. In fact, it is. And yet it is one of the most profound skills leaders require in order to up their game and create real magic in their business.

Get this right and all of a sudden people start coming to you with their exciting new ideas.

You become their Elvis.

DO FAVOURS

Business has a karmic nature. It can take a long time for the seeds you sow to bear fruit.

For example, in sales functions a great deal of effort goes into building relationships that are of no immediate benefit in the expectation of reaping future rewards. You throw your energy out there and you hope that at some point it comes back. When it does come back it's surprising – it's often in disproportionate measure and the timing is anything but predictable.

The same principle exists with the people inside your business. If you help them out in whatever way you can, karma will usually ensure that someday, in some way, you will be repaid.

For many in business the idea of doing anything for anyone that doesn't result in a direct payback seems alien. Those people are missing the point. As I say to my kids constantly, 'Nice brings nice and bad brings bad.'

If you spread happiness around your workplace and put yourself out for others, the goodwill you generate has a value far greater than the effort you expend originally.

Be generous with your time and your help.

Be interested in other people, their struggles and their dreams. You'll find they will be more interested in yours.

When you help somebody, you form a connection with them that is deeper than usual. The more you connect with people, the more chance there is that you'll be noticed, create energy and therefore shine in any business situation.

A favour can be something as simple as making tea for everyone, helping out with a difficult presentation, or offering inspiration to a colleague who is stuck.

I once had a real problem regarding my role in an agency and wasn't sure if I could reconcile it, so was considering resignation. The chairman was on holiday in Devon but he got the board together for dinner with me so we could sort it out – he drove to join us and then returned to his family that night. I have never forgotten that and I have been keen to repay it ever since. Get out from your desk and be abundant with your talents.

Surprise people by helping them when you have no obvious reason to do so, and notice the impact. Karma will reward you in the most unusual and pleasing ways.

BE INTERESTED IN OTHER PEOPLE, THEIR STRUGGLES AND THEIR DREAMS.

(YOU'LL FIND THEY WILL BE MORE INTERESTED IN YOURS.)

MAKE STUFF SIMPLE

The business world sometimes – actually, most of the time – is a self-complicating machine.

If three senior executives are left in a room with a box of matches, a candle and a bottle of wine, you can guarantee an hour later they won't have enjoyed a deeply connecting human conversation and the complex aromas of the vintage. They will have analysed the consumer proposition of romance and worked out its return on investment.

Complicating things is often perceived as clever. It isn't clever, it's stupid. To make things simple you really have to be smart, and it takes a lot more effort than most senior execs ever invest.

People want to understand stuff. We love to comprehend, and yet the language and jargon people use in business seems designed to make that virtually impossible. Not only does this business-speak exclude everyone but those in the club, it also makes some dangerous assumptions. It's a bit like the story of the Emperor's new clothes. When you use a term that isn't absolutely clear to someone, they will rarely question it for fear of appearing stupid.

Keep things simple and you'll never have to worry about people missing your point.

Speak in pictures

Human nature is such that in meetings we often don't want to rock the boat or draw more attention to ourselves, especially when the bosses are in town. If anything unclear is said or shown, chances are that no one will challenge it. So your job as a leader is to communicate in such a way that everybody immediately understands what you mean.

This means avoiding jargon and business-speak.

One way to do this is to use more pictures, metaphors and analogies to grab people's attention.

Tell more stories and bring things to life in such a way that anyone from nine to ninety would understand what you mean.

I recently saw Al Carey, the CEO of snack food giant Frito-Lay, explain the company's mission. It was beautiful. I got it instantly, because he broke his presentation down into simple headlines. Each point had a visual icon, a personal story and a video that made it real. I'm sure it took a huge investment of time and money to make his message so solid, but when you consider the power of getting it right and having the whole business aligned behind that message, it was worth every penny and every drop of sweat.

Ben Rich, the guy who headed up Lockheed's Advanced Development Projects, aka the Skunk Works, needed funding for the F-117 stealth bomber from the CIA during the late 1970s. He did his presentations and showed the maths, but there are only a handful of people on earth who understand what dihedral or trihedral radar plates do. Hence, what would today be the 'PowerPoint' approach wasn't proving to be of any use.

He turned up to the next meeting with nothing under his arm at all; no charts, no figures. The CIA leaders and the Chiefs of Staff all leered at him in disbelief.

Ben took a marble-sized ball bearing from his pocket and rolled it across the desk to the general. 'The plane I can build you has the same size radar profile when it's parked in front of the enemy dish as that ball bearing has in the sky ten miles away from the target.'

He got his funding.

All of us can be more clear. When we keep things simple and real, people 'get' us and what it is that we are driving for. That helps us to shine more brightly and create more impact in business.

Next time you have something to communicate in a meeting, think about how you can do it differently. How can you grab your audience's imagination in a simple and powerful way?

HAVE A THING

Interesting people often have a thing.

It may be that they dress in a particular way.

It may be that they have a passion to try new things.

It may be that every time they have a meeting they make people laugh.

It doesn't really matter what the thing is, but you need one.

Things make us different; things make us interesting. All of that makes us shine.

Get a thing, and then go ding-a-ling with your thing because a thing in a box is not a thing with a ring.

My thing is poetry (obviously).

LEADERSHIP ME, TIMES THREE

To shine you have to lead. Shining by its very essence inspires others to be more and do more. Your influence over your colleagues increases exponentially and so does your leadership potential.

We all have times when we need to help others get to a better solution, whether it be a group or an individual. Those times require us to lead.

We all have our way of being in the world – behaviours and tricks we've picked up that make us feel comfortable and confident. These become habitual. You'll already have a preferred way of leading people, and in many cases I'm sure it's very effective.

To be a bright shiny leader, however, you need to swing three ways. None of these ways are perfect but they each create magic that at times is invaluable.

The first style is forward leadership. This is a traditional form of leadership and involves you having enough expertise to be able to establish a vision and drive from the front, so that others follow. To make this work you need to be confident of what you're doing and where you're going. It's effective when you don't have much time, and when you know your stuff better than those you're leading.

The second style is leadership alongside. This is collaborative leadership, where you help the group decide what it should do and how it should do it, and have an equal share of those decisions. The style suits creative exploration and when you are working with peers. It takes a bit longer but it's great for ownership and thinking differently.

The third style is leading from behind. This involves you coaching the team so that they make all the decisions and have ownership of what happens next. This can take a lot longer but the benefit is that you're transferring capability to them for the future and you don't need to be an expert in the content.

Most pieces of work can benefit from all three of these styles used at the correct stage of their development. When starting a project I spend a long time leading from behind, as I am asking a lot of questions and don't have enough information to do much more than coach my client. Once I've established what the project needs, I often become a forward leader, suggesting how I think we should tackle it. I will then drop to the collaborative style to kick around ideas about how to build on that suggestion. I may have used three styles in a ten-minute period.

Your impact will be enhanced if you are more aware of these styles, and consciously adopt them when the time is right.

If I ever get stuck when working on some new thinking with others, changing my style invariably gets us moving again – more than any other intervention. That's a big resource.

We all have our favourites and we all use them differently, especially when you consider 'content leadership' (what the project is about) versus 'process leadership' (how to do it). So just work out which one feels most natural to you and which one will really enhance your relationships and projects.

In all cases you are leading. It's just that some styles will help you shine more brightly at certain times.

BE IN THE PICTURE

Business needs a clear view of where it is going. You need to make that view relevant to you and to the people you work with.

The best leaders I know are relentless communicators, who always tell stories about the things that are most important to the business at that time. These stories soon become a part of company legend and culture.

If you want to stand out from the crowd, make sure you know where things are going, and tell good stories to illustrate it.

Populate your stories with people you want to make heroes of. The finance director who saved a million. The PA who saved her boss's bacon by spotting a flaw in his plan. The engineer who fiddled with an idea over many weekends that ended up being the next innovation. Every time you tell that story you give your characters more energy and more chance to shine.

In the same way, make sure there are some stories featuring you. Just as you tell stories about others, others will tell stories about you. And there is nothing better than being part of the business's projected future to make sure you stand out from the crowd.

To make these stories really effective, align them to your company's strategic goals. You have to tell a tale that is both simple and memorable, one that creates an emotional response and ends with a clear outcome that is all the richer for having you involved.

It works best if the stories aren't overtly self-promoting, but instead show you in a positive light in comparison with the values of the business. For example, if your business thrust is all about taking more risk, tell a story of how you did just that and got it wrong … yet your boss remained supportive because you were trying to follow the business's commitment to a portfolio approach.

Tell stories, and paint a picture of the future – but make sure you're in it.

DO SOMETHING PHYSICAL

I have been struck over the years by how many business leaders have some type of obsessive commitment to physical activity.

Lots of them love running, swimming, going to the gym or riding their ever-so-fancy bicycles. There are those obsessed by gardening, their vegetable patches or home renovation. Very few would choose sitting on the sofa over sailing a yacht, or lying in bed over hiking up a mountain.

One of L'Oréal's executives shared a leadership insight with me that I could relate to completely: to balance out our energies, we need to do something with our hands.

We spend far too much of our time exercising our minds and little else. Yet the human blueprint is not simply to be a walking brain; we are designed as physical beasts. Our extraordinary processing power sets us apart from the rest of the animal kingdom, but it has upset the balance between what we do with our brains and our bodies, and it's our bodies that help us manage our energies.

Many hard-working execs hit the gym or play squash to restore the balance. When our brains are used so much more than our bodies we need something to help us process the emotions of the day. One of the simplest ways of doing this is to go for a run. Some years ago I used to run home from work. It was about five miles and, being the lazy runner that I am, it would take me a good fifty minutes of running through Hyde Park and some of the busiest streets in London. By the time I was at home I had released everything from my day and was in the right state to be a husband and a father.

We all need to release energy on a regular basis. Otherwise it gets stored up and comes out in unpredictable, dangerous and damaging ways.

Recently I have become drawn to activities that involve creation and growth. There is nothing like surrounding ourselves with the beauty of nature and doing something physical to connect ourselves to it. For many years I could never understand why some people love gardening and now I'm spookily attracted by it. Perhaps this explains the obsessiveness of golfers. There must be more to the game than hitting a little ball into a little hole and dressing like a pimp; it must also be about the joy of walking and chatting in nature's own living room.

Make sure there is some type of release for you, so that your body can enjoy being alive and vital as much as your overdeveloped and overused brain.

EVERYTHING IS ENERGY

Consider your business life as an electrical circuit.

When you take on any task or project, you channel energy into that circuit. It has resistance and impedance, which means the energy will dissipate as it circulates. The bigger and more complex the circuit, the more resistance it has.

So how can you use your limited energy for maximum returns? Be smart in where you deploy it, and in limiting resistance.

First, only use your energy on things you believe in. It is much harder to generate energy when your heart isn't in it. When you believe in something your energy is greater, goes further and has more impact. If you don't believe in what you're doing, stop.

Secondly, create waterslides. At a theme park, water-slides are fast and fun. There is so much latent energy and such a lack of friction. You hurtle down and fly out with a big smile on your face. You can apply the same principle in business.

Every piece of work can be designed as a waterslide (as opposed to a hike up the Himalayas, dragging three suitcases and an elderly relative behind you).

To do this, you need to anticipate where resistance is likely to occur and take steps to minimize it. Think ahead and read the mood of those who will oppose you.

If you are trying to have a project approved, moved or funded, there's usually somebody who can make it hard for you. Or, if you're lucky, there might be someone who can smooth the path. Either way, you can have a one-on-one conversation with them before the formal meeting. That little chat will help to build a waterslide.

If you add in a connection between your project and the core strategy of the business, your CEO's pet ambition, and a recent customer need that everyone is buzzing about, the waterslide starts to get steeper and smoother. Not only are you still going with the flow, you are making the flow even stronger to make sure that your project slides right along with it.

I am one of those annoying people who loves starting projects but soon gets bored and moves onto the next one. To counter this deficiency I've surrounded myself with people who are able to finish the things I start. I have also designed my life so that most of my impact is made in short sharp blasts, rather than planning things I know will eventually become tedious.

I make sure that I start something new and fun on a regular basis to keep that part of me satisfied. Of course, such projects have to be in line with where I want my business to go, but I am less tough on the criteria for success and have set aside funds to throw at them with no expectation of a return (even though they always seem to be profitable). I am therefore working with the energy rather than fighting against it. My waterslides are nicely designed for me.

What will yours look like?

KNOW WHAT YOU NEED

All we really need to survive are food and water, shelter and love. But to really shine brightly, we need a little bit more.

When looking back at your life, you'll notice certain times when you took more risk, had more fun and were more 'you'. Usually those times were fuelled by something important to you, something you needed.

It may be that you need to be doing some good in this world, or that you need to be training people, or that you need to be in a wildly competitive environment. We're all slightly different, but we have to know what those things are that make us tick.

Think of times when you have been really livid, when you've felt that something or someone was just plain wrong, or that something close to your heart was challenged or offended. Write down at least five of them.

Read today's newspapers. What stories create a negative reaction in you: tension, anger or sadness? What is it that creates such emotion? What is it that's being threatened that you value so highly?

When I did this exercise recently I found I'd been most frustrated when my actions hadn't had any impact and I was wasting my time, when I was not learning, and when I felt I didn't have space to do new things.

Now think of times when your heart has soared. When you felt that you were in the right place at the right time doing the right thing. It might have been at work, with your family or just something you love. What is it about these times that feel so good to you?

Mine included working with people who challenged me, periods when I had time and space to create, and producing something that is visible to the world.

By exploring these occasions you can build a clear idea of what is important to you. These elements need to show up in the work you do, and how you do it, if you are going to tap into your real power and dynamism.

By aligning your work to the circumstances you enjoy most, you will be guaranteed to tap into extra oomph!

BACK TO BASICS

Life is too full.

We are bombarded by messages from the omnipresent media.

We juggle so many roles and duties.

We live fast and feel uncomfortable when we are quiet and still.

Although we have become fabulous multitaskers, we have grown further removed from our essence as sensitive beings. With all this stimulus it's impossible to listen to what's going on inside while noticing the opportunities on the outside.

To recalibrate, take a little holiday from your life.

Cut back on everything – media, phones, tasks and obligations. I even cut out cooked food, caffeine and booze, which for me is a huge distraction. A week on salads and fresh fruit juice is a great life-detox.

After a week, add the things back that you consciously choose: not the ones that you have been hard wired to do, but the ones that are good for your soul.

Life will be lighter, more attuned and back under your control. Rinse and repeat every few months.

STANDARDS, MY DEAR, STANDARDS

After training thousands of people to be better innovators, I have a clear view on what leads to success and what leads to mediocrity. The distinguishing factor is not talent, role or even ambition: it is standards.

We all live life to our own standards. Those standards dictate the impact we have. In business, the variance in standards from colleague to colleague is obvious.

It's not just about how dedicated you are to preparing your PowerPoint deck or any other core output of your role. What matter are the standards by which you interact with others, manage your relationships and help create energy in the business.

It's the people stuff that is the key to shining.

On the face of it, it's a lot easier to have low standards; to run sloppy meetings and give half-baked reviews. It takes less effort and talent to amble through business life. But by doing so you will never shine – you will always be average, at best. If you put in the extra effort to make sure your interactions have output, that concerns voiced by your people are dealt with, and that your meetings are crisp and engaging, your impact will soar. To do so you need to maintain high standards.

I was recently helping out on a project between two of the world's biggest brands. The facilitators had done a great job in setting up an environment that would really help creativity flourish. Even so, some senior people in the middle of group sessions would pick up their BlackBerries and be distracted by the outside world. This is a classic example of both low standards and ignorance of their impact. They were great people but had become sloppy about how they conducted themselves.

A great leader knows that the little things they do have a big impact on the psyche of the business. Those things include never keeping people waiting, being genuinely interested in what people have to say, upholding commitments, setting the context clearly in any interaction and sharing themselves even when they have been working flat-out for weeks. Those are the standards that help people shine.

What are the standards that you are committed to

that resonate highly, fit you as a brand and have most impact on the work that you do? What can people count on you for?

BE CONSISTENT, BE INCONSISTENT

One of the reasons standards are so important is that people know what they can rely on you to do. Once they know that, they find it easier to engage with you and to make the most of your talents. Flaky business folk aren't liked by anyone because all they do is increase the level of risk.

As a leader, you need to be consistent in the way that you perform. People need to know what to expect from you each time they approach you.

The more closely aligned that is with what's important to you and the brand that you are, the more chance that it will be amplified into the business. Great brands are consistent in all they do; the same needs to be true of you and your brand.

The only downside with consistency is that it is dull. So you also need to make sure there are some areas in your business life which are inconsistent and surprising.

It might mean that every month you do a bit of experimenting with something core to your business. Or maybe you ring the changes on certain aspects of business life that have become stale.

Keep people on their toes and the level of energy and engagement goes up, giving you more of their genius, and helping you once again to shine bright.

YOU HAVE A CHOICE: YOU ARE FREE

You can do anything you want. Anything at all.

I know that point of view can easily be dismissed as idealistic, but it's a reality. You are limited only by your imagination.

In my early days in business I went to a workshop that offered me one particularly useful piece of advice. They told me that I should save money for a 'fuck-it fund'.

I loved the idea as it felt quite naughty, especially as the business that employed me paid for that advice.

I put some cash away over the years and eventually I got to the stage where I knew the job I was in was not what I wanted, and yet had no idea which job should be next. Without my little 'fuck-it fund' I would not have had the choice to throw it in and go exploring.

Or would I?

That money gave me the confidence to do something bold. I didn't really need to have a bucket of cash to do that – it was just a handy safety net.

The business world has changed enormously. There are no rules as to how we are employed and how we make money. Most of my friends and people I do business with are no longer employed, or if they are it is with numerous organizations. We now have the opportunity to create the life we want, by helping our business activities flex around who we are and what we need.

It is crucial for our mental and emotional health to know that we don't need the job we are in. We can do something else, and do it well.

Therefore you should only do the job you do if it's what you want and it's giving you what you need. You have a choice, and it's important to realize that, because when you do, you do things for the right reasons and enjoy the sense of liberation. It makes it easier to take risks, easier to speak your mind and do what you believe in. It makes it easier for you to be you every day when you work, and not just toe the line as a corporate professional.

I know mothers who work three days a week during term time and then spend the rest of the time with their children. When they're working they are fresh and full of energy, and when they're not working they are great mothers because they can give their full attention to their children.

One of my colleagues at Upping Your Elvis is also employed by The Mind Gym and runs his own business. A fresher man is hard to find.

The message is not that you have to get a new job to get what you need – it's that you can if you want. Once you realize that, you are more likely to get what you need from the job you already have.

You bring more magic to your work when you know you're doing it because you want to, not because you have to. It gives you an edge and confidence that can really rile incompetent leaders; they need you but you don't need them, and knowing that means they have to work much harder to keep you happy.

I ran a workshop ten years ago that led to eight out of nine delegates getting new jobs within a year. Most employers hated it as they had lost good talent.

But one employer had a completely different take. He believed that if people need to move on, they should. That it was a natural part of the career cycle and that all employers should be encouraging people to be all they could be. If he couldn't offer that, he should free them. Quite the visionary.

You are free. Enjoy it!

SURROUND YOURSELF WITH TALENT, AND BE MERCILESS

Once upon a time leaders in business felt a little bit like a jealous bride. 'If my bridesmaids are too pretty, who will notice me on my big day?' I am sure that less confident leaders feel the same now. 'If my team is too talented, and they look too good, then I'll look average.'

It's a classic example of playing small when you could play huge.

If you really want to shine brightly and set this world on fire, surround yourself with talent that scares you.

Never worry that they may take your job, because that's just what you should want them to do. If they don't take your job you'll never move on and be as fantastic as you can be. You should be begging for them to take your role so that you can find a better one.

We can't do everything and we certainly can't be experts in all the skills that we would love to master. That's why we need great talent around us to plug the gaps and help with the heavy lifting. We will never develop unless we have superstars all around us, and we will never be able to get the headspace we need for new thinking unless the day-to-day stuff is left confidently in the hands of our protégés.

To keep that standard so high you must be merciless. I don't mean in a Genghis Khan style, but you must never allow yourself any slack when it comes to your judgements on people and how well you coach, support and develop them.

I once made a corking mistake. I had set up a new company with my then business partner and we had ambitions to take over the world. We took on our first recruit – let's call her Eve – and were overexcited about her talent. Eve came with us to our first project and at the end of it we had a quick chat in the taxi on the way home. My partner and I both agreed that she was a bit odd, but we were sure that 'she'd be OK'.

A year or so later the team had grown to almost twenty people and Eve was still posing something of a problem. We never really worried about it because everyone else was so good. Then she did something so off-values that the whole team recoiled. It turned out that the team had never thought Eve fitted in and had spent a lot of time covering up her performance and resenting it. Once she'd gone they more than happily shared her work among themselves, and once again the team smelt of roses.

The mistake was that we had spotted the potential problem with Eve at the outset but had ignored it, which then sent out a signal to everybody that it was fine to be difficult and contrary.

Since that day I have made myself apply ruthless standards to the talent around me. I never chicken out and say that someone 'will be OK', because OK is not the standard that my clients would hold me to. Being ruthless means also being clear on what you are recruiting for and how you discover that in people. I used to hold 'on your feet' sessions for potential talent where we could see how well candidates could hold a room and engage a group. We would know in minutes whether an individual was right for us or not, and more accurately than from any number of interviews.

Another example of making it real with recruitment was when we were looking to hire two new creative coordinators whose job would be to stage-manage projects – helping to ensure that everything ran smoothly in terms of organization, props and stimulus etc. The team doing the hiring had shortlisted the hottest eight applicants and invited them all to a half-day 'get to know you better' session in the office.

Just as the session was about to begin, the potential recruits were all sitting comfortably on the sofas, waiting for things to start, and in walked the recruiters, each with an armful of paper and pens. One of them tripped, sending pens flying everywhere. All the potential recruits looked on apart from two, who instinctively jumped to their feet and helped pick up the Bics.

The whole thing had been staged, of course, to discover who was the most likely to pile in and help without having to be asked. It was no longer an intellectual assessment; the recruiters had seen for themselves.

It doesn't end with the handshake

One of the best recruiters I've met is Dan Walker, who was the head of talent at Apple.

Dan coined the phrase 'It's better to have a hole than an arsehole'. Never was a truer talent philosophy ever expressed and then proven by my own painful experience with Eve.

Dan had incredible resources and tons of experience and yet he still believed he was right only 50 per cent of the time at best. So I have to believe that most of us would have an even lower strike rate. The most important period of any employee's recruitment is their first three months at work. This is the time when you can make a proper on-the-job assessment of their talent and shape their whole way of working to fit what your business needs from them. I can now tell if someone will be successful by working with them during their first week.

You must live with your new recruits, give them feedback constantly and see how they respond to it. If they hear nothing about their performance and how they fit in until three months later, you have just wasted the most perfect opportunity you can have as a leader: the chance to take somebody fresh and energized and tap their talents.

No one should be too busy to hang out with new recruits. No one should think that they become valued only after they have been in the business for a year or two. Their naïveté is what makes new recruits golden.

Dan also believed that reviews and appraisals were a waste of time. I ran a team for whom the formalized review process was simply a summary of the conversations that they'd had during the previous twelve months. My people continually reviewed themselves by recording their feedback from everyone else in the business, summarizing it at year end and then playing it back to me. I rarely had to add much to their self-assessments as they owned the themes in them so completely: they were telling me, as opposed to me telling them. If people didn't know how well they were doing, it was my fault and my fault alone.

A self-reviewing and self-developing organization is incredibly powerful. But it will only work if you put talent above all else and your investment in them above yourself. You have to believe.

NEVER HAVE TO REMEMBER

I hate having to remember things. It takes up far too much of my headspace to make it of any value. I also don't make notes, because making notes prevents me from listening with both my ears and my eyes, noticing what people really mean when their bodies tell me a different story from their mouths.

So I have a challenge. How can I be successful in business when I don't want to have to remember and I don't want to take notes?

My first principle is never to write anything down

because note taking soon becomes habitual and stops you listening properly. When you don't write things down, your mind focuses on the headlines.

My brain then filters out the chat and stores only the stuff that's important, which is usually much less than would have been written on the page. I know if it's a contract negotiation the detail needs to be set down somewhere, but for 98 per cent of my time writing is a distraction.

If something is really important I put it in my diary to remind me, but even that is usually a waste of effort. Often, when the day arrives, it's no longer that important. And if it is, I'll probably have remembered it anyway.

Information is everywhere; insight is not. Experiment with approaches and systems that allow you to focus on delivering the insight and not on managing endless reams of information.

When I first decided not to remember, I had to train myself for many months to let certain things out of my head and to feel relaxed about not having every fact at my fingertips. One way that I did this was to act immediately when something needed doing. So if I was in a conversation and we agreed to set up a meeting with a third party, I would do it there and

IMMEDIATE ACTION KEEPS YOUR MIND CLEAR AND YOUR TO-DO LIST TINY.

then. Immediate action keeps your mind clear and your to-do list tiny.

When you combine this approach with focusing on the One Big Thing you need to do each day, life becomes incredibly simple. The big stuff happens.

DIARY NEVERLAND

Most people feel they have no control over time. There never seem to be enough hours in the day. Very often this is due to ridiculous office scheduling.

There's a fantasy that if you book a meeting from 9 a.m. until 10 a.m., you can then begin a meeting at 10 a.m. somewhere else in the business. No wonder everyone seems stressed out and behind the '8' ball. Just to satisfy their schedule they need to have mastered time travel (expenses are hard enough, let alone teleporting).

The way a meeting starts is often how it finishes. If it starts late and floppy it is almost impossible to keep the standard of interaction high. Therefore if you have a 10 a.m. meeting, it needs to start at 10 a.m.

To achieve this you need to make your schedule realistic. In reality your 9 a.m. meeting cannot last one hour. It should last forty-five minutes. That forty-five minutes is a good amount of time – it's about as far as you can push somebody and keep their concentration to optimum level. You just need to be punchier to get things done more quickly.

So at 9.45 a.m. you end the meeting and spend five minutes reviewing what you've learned and how to make the next meeting even better. You then high-five and dance your way to the next venue, allowing five minutes to get there.

(If your campus is large, you might need to adjust your travelling times, but you get the point.)

You can then arrive at your 10 a.m. meeting five minutes early, with ample opportunity to score a mocha chocolate latte, shuffle some paper, exchange pleasantries and be ready to start at the top of the hour. And if everyone adopts your wonderful working practice, you know the meeting room will have been available for five minutes before you arrived.

All right, it sounds basic, but the level of stress that can be created in a business by nonsensical scheduling is bizarrely masochistic.

And don't even get me started on this 'I'm so senior, people wait for me' rubbish. What that means is, 'I don't care what the impact is on the little people in this company, because my time is far more important.' Get over yourself!

If anyone says, 'I can attend your meeting for the first ten minutes but then I have to go', your answer is quite simply: 'Then don't come at all.'

You haven't got time for passengers. It has to be all or nothing. Certain individuals do this a lot as it attracts attention to them and makes them feel more in control. What a sad way to get it. Just manage your time and life gets shinier. People will thank you for ever.

Rant over.

LIE DOWN WHEN YOU CAN

I was once working with the board of the American confectionery company Hershey's. One of the directors told me that he meditates every afternoon. For some reason I was surprised (it may have been his cowboy boots).

Meditation may not be that common in Western business, but it has served generations brilliantly in the East. If I'm working on a book, speech or some new workshop content, I spend a lot of time lying down. Invariably when I do so, I acquire a breakthrough in my thinking; a new perspective, new insight, or a startling revelation.

When we relax we start to access our subconscious. It helps us de-stress and gives us an energy boost, but more importantly it helps release our creative genius.

Winston Churchill recommended taking a nap every afternoon, and not an armchair nap but a take-all-your-clothes-off-and-get-into-bed nap. He was adamant that this meant you would achieve more in your day. I agree. The practicalities of twenty-first-century working life mean that slipping between 800 thread-count Egyptian sheets mid-afternoon may be a challenge. However, there are many ways that we can access a relaxed state without putting on our jim-jams.

You can go for a walk and switch off your mobile. Just stroll and ponder for at least twenty minutes.

Or find a quiet space, sit straight, feet on the floor, take a deep breath and smile. Notice how easy it is for you to relax.

I know people who lie down underneath their desks for fifteen minutes after lunch. It's a shame that so many people would find that unprofessional, when in reality it means that they can perform to a much higher level for the whole afternoon.

Some firms are blazing a trail with chill-out zones, nap rooms and even hammock gardens. Those with enough office space are bringing in daybeds and are often found upon them, flicking through their weekly reports.

Be confident in using relaxation to help you tap your creativity. Business will never feel quite the same. And everyone will be jealous as hell.

THE RABBIT HOLE OF E-MAIL

E-mail is fantastic – an incredible advance in enabling the world to connect.

As we all know, however, it is used to excess in ways that are unhealthy. When a communication medium becomes as prolific as e-mail we stop thinking about other options and in a knee-jerk reaction go straight to the keyboard.

If you really want to shine in business, choose to communicate in other, more advantageous ways.

One of the problems with any written communication is that printed words can easily be misinterpreted. They lack the rich variations in tonality, pitch and cadence of the spoken voice; and indeed the sensory indulgence of meeting face to face.

If your communication is anything but transactional, go to the phone or go to the person. This is the way that relationships are built; this is the way you can shine more brightly.

Unless you're a literary genius, it is tricky to be distinctive via e-mail. Even if you are, there is no guarantee that people will read it in the right state.

There's a renaissance in letter writing, of which I am a great fan. When people receive a letter it's as if a magical gift has been bestowed upon them; when it is handwritten, the sorcery enchants them. I recently received a letter of thanks from a Director General in the British government. I have kept it somewhere safe; it lives on.

If you want people to take notice and appreciate your personal touch, write to them on paper. And use a nice pen.

HAVE KILLER NUMBERS

When you dig down to the basics, most businesses are all about numbers.

Regardless of how right-on or wrinkly the leadership is, no matter how awesomely they empower their teams, everyone gets their real buzz from seeing good numbers.

Good numbers are those that either ratify their strategy or help them come up with the next smart one. Numbers mean clever, and clever means prizes.

When I was working on Carling Black Label ... Let me rephrase that: When I was marketing Carling Black Label lager I remember being in the smoking room in the London headquarters of Carling's parent company, Bass plc. I was with my friend and then boss Andy Fennell, now chief marketing officer of the drinks giant Diageo. Sir Ian Prosser, at the time CEO of Bass, also liked a puff. He was someone we'd so far rarely managed to meet, but on this day our shared addiction to carcinogens meant we could strike up some happy banter.

When Sir Ian asked how Carling was doing, Andy threw him a number that demonstrated huge gains over Budweiser, a rival brand that Carling particularly wanted to do well against. Sir Ian was excited as it was a very good number indeed, and he was about to sign off the annual report for shareholders.

The rest of the day was spent making sure that number was bulletproof. It went into the report and added a bit of razzle-dazzle for all who read it.

Andy knows the power of numbers. In that moment he managed to have a profound impact on the most senior person in the business by having a good number to give him. And not just a good number, but the best good number. He could have offered any one of a hundred other interesting statistics; the trick is to find those that are sexy and back up your strategic focus.

To really shine, always carry three good numbers around with you.

The best numbers are those that few people have access to or are aware of. They are ones that guarantee a big impact – usually surprise and intrigue. 'Really? That's interesting, tell me more' is the reaction you want.

I was recently working on a project with the Nike Foundation and the Department for International

Development and someone gave me this number: 'Teenage girls will invest 90 per cent of their wealth in their families as opposed to 30 to 40 per cent for boys.' Now those are good numbers, numbers with power. They can be the basis of a strategy that can change the lives of millions.

BE A BRAND

Imagine that you are a washing powder on a supermarket shelf. You need to stand out to be chosen. If you are bland and stand for nothing, then no one will pick you up. If, however, there is something unique about you, at least you will attract attention. If that uniqueness is what people want, then you will end up in the shopping basket.

A similar analogy can be made at work.

Decisions are made every day that influence our future. These may concern the work we do, the breaks we get, the opportunities that give us a chance to get on. What getting on means to you may be very different from what it means to me. Whether it's about money, fame, lifestyle, excitement or being allocated the next big project, it comes from being at the top of the list in the minds of the people who give you those breaks.

The way to stay at the top is to shine. The more Elvis you are at work, the more breaks you'll get, and thus the more Elvis you'll become. Elvis was pretty sure of what he stood for. He had trademarks that everyone recognized and a set of clearly defined talents. That was what made him shine.

To stand out, you need to be a consistent and reliable brand; a product that anyone is happy to have in their basket. To do that takes effort. It's much easier to be shaped by the environment than to shape yourself.

To become a saleable brand you need to be single-minded, committed and clear. A brand's best qualities come to the fore when things are tough, and so should yours. To weather the storm you need to be absolutely sure of who you are and why you stand for what you do, otherwise the storm will smudge your lines and make you bland, head down bracing against the wind.

Not only do you need to be a distinctive brand, but that brand has to radiate attributes that add benefit to your organization. You need to be able to create value, think differently and see opportunities. You need to be capable of harnessing the potential of what's around you and have a restless energy for challenging the norm. That's what Elvises do.

I used to know someone who worked at Coca-Cola. He was an extraordinary brand within a very hierarchical and conservative culture. He had long hair, never shaved during the week and always wore black. His office was filled with art.

Not only did he visually stand out, he had ways of being that were incredibly distinct. If you met him, there was no doubt you would remember him.

He might not have been to everyone's taste but he certainly attracted attention and energy, more than those around him on equal pegging. He stood for something and he stood out.

Make sure you do too.

DO WHAT YOU LOVE
AND ARE GREAT AT

This is the best advice I was ever given.

If you are great at what you do, it sets you apart and is your route to riches.

If you love what you do, you will have more energy to devote to your passion than those who do not, and therefore you will become even better at it.

Each day you will have to pinch yourself to realize that you really are living the dream. It becomes effortless and fills your soul.

BE A GROWN-UP, HAVE A CHAT

Naturally, people fall out. Businesses are hotbeds of contention and exist harmoniously only as a freak snapshot in time. There are always relationship issues, because we are human and that's what makes life interesting.

I recently returned from a long business trip on an overnight flight that landed on a Saturday morning. When I got home I spent some time with my children and swapped stories with my wife. Over breakfast she said that she'd arranged to take the kids and some of their friends to the park and would be back mid-afternoon.

I felt awful. After being away for so long, it felt as if my wife was taking away the thing I so badly needed: family time. She noticed and asked what was the matter. I explained that I had been looking forward to some good family time and she began to giggle. This could have been the start of a major row, but we had a good talk about our different perspectives on the situation.

I thought that my wife didn't want to be with me, which was most unfair since I had been away for a week working hard making money so we could feed our little monkeys. My wife thought that she was doing me a favour by taking them out for a few hours, giving me time to take a shower, unpack and have a nap, so that for the rest of the weekend I could be the best daddy in the world.

She was trying to help me hit the very objective that I was striving for, yet it seemed to us both that the other had a very different agenda.

Similar misunderstandings arise every day in business. Somebody does something that we interpret one way and yet we never really trouble ourselves to discover what their thinking really is. So many hours and days are wasted because those grown-up conversations are not happening, and much childish sulking is generated as a result.

To shine brightly in business, your relationships need to be super-buffed and squeaky clean.

I spent eighteen months researching innovation projects to understand what it was that created success or failure. So many died before their value was close to being realized. I found that eight out of ten times when a project floundered, it was because a tricky conversation didn't take place.

Pressure valves

In reality there need be no such thing as a tricky conversation: we just imagine them to be so, and avoid them like the plague. You feel fantastic after most such conversations because they take the pressure out of the situation and help people get along.

The conversation should follow exactly the same process as what I described earlier as funky feedback (see page 119). The principle of sorting out relationships is the same as for making feedback useful. You have to isolate the facts and then own your interpretations.

I recently did some work for a client but hadn't been paid after the agreed period of thirty days. This client was also a friend of mine and I didn't want money to become an issue. So this is how the conversation went.

'Hey, Jack, got a moment to talk about my payment for the gig I did three months ago?'

'Sure thing, what is it?'

'Well, I did it three months ago and invoiced you immediately, but I still haven't received payment, which is way beyond our thirty-day terms.'

'Yes, that's true.'

'My interpretation is that your company policy is to spin it for as long as possible, thus enhancing your cash flow, and I guess it's now in the hands of your finance people. I feel frustrated because I did a great job with fantastic feedback and therefore feel undervalued. I'm not sure I want to do the next gig that we've got booked in.'

Jack then shared his interpretation, which was a surprising one to me. He had signed off the work and yet hadn't yet gained his board's approval for the payment. So the reason I hadn't been paid had nothing to do with the finance department; it was that Jack had been dragging his heels getting my invoice passed. He suggested I send two invoices over the next two months, each for 50 per cent of the total. He could then sign them off immediately, making me a happy boy and keeping our relationship straight and true.

By being absolutely clear on fact and supposition we can remain aligned and make sure we're supporting each other. The fantasies from the deep never rise to the surface.

This approach has saved thousands of business relationships, not to mention untold marriages. By bringing our interpretations into the light of day and owning them, while knowing that they may be incorrect, we have a chance to truly show ourselves, offer up some vulnerability and be willing to make things work with colleagues.

Is there anyone in your life with whom your relationship is not as good as you'd like it to be? What is driving that disaffection? Plan out the conversation that you would like to have with that person in order to help you get back into the groove.

Remember, you have to be in a good state to have this conversation. If you are angry or nervous, you are taking it too personally.

Take the perspective that there is no such thing as a bad person, just actions that you don't appreciate. Those actions are not right or wrong, they just are. It's your job to make sense of them by having a conversation, so you can then take control of that process.

As long as your intention is honest, and you are committed to improving your relationship, you can only do good.

ADMIN ALCHEMY

Not every part of any job can be sexy and fun. We all have endless admin to complete, and tasks that don't fit our personal style.

We have to do those things but we can make them more energized. Schedule a time that fits the task.

Find a way of doing the things you dislike in a way that's more fun, faster, amusing, rewarding, and then minimize the amount of time you spend on them.

Delegate admin tasks. Swap them with colleagues who enjoy them while you take on some of their troublesome tasks that are better suited to you.

Talk to your boss. Explain those areas in which you're hopeless and ask if you could spend more time doing things that you are wonderful at.

Redesigning your role will rapidly improve your pain versus pleasure balance.

And if it doesn't … go and do something else.

Sssssshhhhh!

STOP TALKING – LISTEN!
(SILENCE IS REALLY GOLDEN)

You are driving me nuts. Shut up and listen!

It's as if people these days are so over-stimulated by music, TV, YouTube, that when they aren't plugged in to a stimulus they become talking juke boxes.

Sssssshhhhh! Listen to others; listen to yourself. Notice what's on the inside.

People who talk constantly are rarely aware of anything. Most gurus are happy to stay quiet.

Love the silence.

<u>NOT JUST WORK</u>

To build good relationships we need to be more ourselves and emerge from our business identities. No matter how real you try to keep it, people will only ever see your business persona if they only ever see you in at work. To break that pattern, do some human things together with your colleagues and your clients.

Businesses should encourage people to get lots of stimulus into their lives. So why don't you make that happen and benefit from the human connection?

Over the years I have taken part in all sorts of activities with fellow businessmen: wing walking, abseiling, wine tasting, swimming with dolphins, cooking an eight-course meal, sailing, going to the theatre, Bollywood dancing, storytelling, reiki, decorating a school and making music from industrial waste (don't ask).

None of those activities were designed to be any more than great bonding experiences. Yes, a few gave us some insight into some project or other we were working on, but most importantly they all gave us an insight into each other.

There is obviously a time investment, and these things don't come free, but by doing things together you become more connected, more honest and more supportive, making you a better functioning organization.

There is something special about cooking for each other and breaking bread together. It takes minimal time and can be delivered with the most frugal budgets. Buy a chef's hat and make some friends.

GETTING UNSTUCK

We all get stuck. Whether it's a dearth of ideas, the inability to make things happen, or even writer's block, being stuck is part of being alive. So what's the trick to getting back on track?

It's simple: change something.

Remember, your state is simply 'how you are' at any given time; it fluctuates depending on what is going on around and inside you. Your thoughts, clothes, conversations – all affect your state.

And your state itself then influences how you perform, even more than your ability. Strong words, yes, but consider sport. Great athletes who lose their state can perform appallingly, while average athletes who manage their state do well.

By knowing how to manipulate your state, every day becomes more productive, more effortless, more in flow.

Usually, being stuck is not a reality, it's just a state of mind. But the word we choose for that state is telling. In its literal sense, 'stuck' means physically paralysed. Fortunately, that is rarely the case. By moving your body you can change that state of mind, thus becoming unstuck in every sense. Similarly, you can 'move' your mind to another place.

Some of my favourite physical state breakers are walking, running, fresh air, cool water, music, a massage, cutting the hedge.

For a mental spruce-up, picture your loved ones in your mind's eye, think about all the great stuff in your life, or look forward to what you are going to do at the weekend.

FEED THE MACHINE

As a hedonist, I have always known that my body is party central. It's where the good feelings live and is my connection to food, wine, the earth and my loved ones. It's also where I get my energy from.

When I am healthy, vital and strong there is no end to what I can achieve. My mind is then also healthy and my emotions heightened.

When I don't listen to my body and run it into the ground with work, late nights and food designed for comfort rather than sustenance, everything soon falls apart.

Weirdly, with all the riches of our generation, our nutrition and health regimes haven't followed suit. We are growing obese, stressed and desensitized to what we need. We don't need a double-shot cappuccino in the morning to give us energy; we just need a better night's sleep.

Happiness and pleasure are very different things. All too often, short bursts of pleasure are used to fill a more significant happiness hole. Note everything you consume over a working day and see if you are really helping your body be all it can be, or whether you feed it little hits of pleasure to get you through the day. Those pleasure hits will eventually ruin the wonderful machine you were born with. Look after it well.

KILLING FEAR

Fear has a bad rap. 'Fear holds us back; fear stops us from being all we can be' is a refrain we hear constantly from the self-help industry.

Yet fear is there to protect us. A little fear is not a bad thing; too much of it can be crippling. As human beings it's useful to be scared of lions, heights and guns. In these cases, fear could save our lives.

Few of us are exposed to such dangers on a regular basis nowadays, but our survival instincts remain infuriatingly active, sometimes finding the most curious hazards to be frightened of in their place. Fear is created by our minds and plumbed straight into our primal mechanisms. The number one fear in the US is public speaking – greater even than death. I am certain death has more wide-reaching implications than forgetting our words or developing a stammer.

Fear is largely perceptual. What we believe will be scary becomes so. Weirdly, fear and excitement feel very similar, we just label them differently. Time for a re-badging?

What fears are holding you back? What could you overcome with a little change in perspective? You are free to choose your fears; which ones serve you and which ones cripple?

One of my fears is leading a wasteful life. I can view this either as a negative source of concern or as one of the best possible motives to get off my bum and get stuff done. I choose the latter.

FEAR IS LARGELY **PERCEPTUAL.** WHAT WE BELIEVE WILL BE SCARY BECOMES SO.

NICE TRUMPS NASTY

When given a choice to be nice or nasty, choose nice. The energy of positivity will always trump that of negativity.

I once made a trip to Boston to run a couple of days with the Pearson publishing group with a friend, Matt White. Matt has a special skill: he makes people feel great. For two days we took turns to see whose lives we could touch in a positive way – everybody from the cab driver to the receptionist to the bellboy to the barman. It was infectious.

All we really did was be positive with them, helpful, playful, charming and interested. It had to be genuine, and it was. You can't force it. When we left the town the send-off was fantastic and we felt as if we had made some great connections. The whole trip had more purpose and more soul than most I have experienced.

On some days I truly spread the love, while on other days I don't. The times I don't are when I am preoccupied with myself, worrying about something that has yet to happen and trapped in my own head.

On the days that I am there for people and spreading sunshine into their lives, I feel great. In fact, if I start the day in a negative, self-obsessed place and I turn my attention to others and take genuine interest in them, I feel much better about myself.

In business, the energy is often machine-like and functional. By spreading some laughter you connect in a more human way and create shininess around you.

CHECKING IN

If I ask people how they are, I generally get the same answer: 'Good, thanks.' It has nothing to do with reality. They'd probably say the same if they were dying.

There are two reasons for that. The first is that it's not seen as acceptable to give a response that is even vaguely negative; the second is that most people have no clue how they are.

If we don't know how we are, how can we aspire to be better? How can we manage ourselves so that in business we perform to our top level? To improve that awareness, I break 'how we are' down into four main energies.

The first is physical energy. Generally we are more aware of this than the others. When it's depleted we tend to turn to coffee and doughnuts, or sabotage ourselves and then feel hung-over. When we feel physically fantastic, we have power.

The second is mental energy. This often gives us the most trouble. The way we perceive ourselves and the world dictates how we are; if our perceptions warp, we are blocked from being as good as we could be. Our mental energy can be noisy, muddled and fixated on one outcome, making it impossible to be anything more than average. Or it can be focused, clear and open to possibility – which then enables us to be extraordinary.

The third is emotional energy. Emotions are felt in the body, and then interpreted by our mind. We need to be in a good space to achieve new things, so you need to feel happy, excited, optimistic, not depressed or anxious.

The fourth is spiritual energy. This appears on the business agenda far too infrequently; it's the major lever in releasing our potential. It's a sense of connection to you, your values, and the people you're working with.

We are very aware of our spiritual energy when it peaks. When you've worked hard to do something you believe in, and it's suddenly achieved, everything stops. There is peace in the air. A second feels like for ever. Sounds, smells, tastes are stronger. Everything feels possible.

I experience spiritual energy when sailing a boat in a high wind, feeling connected to the water and the gusts in the sails. Or after walking up a mountain and sitting on top of the world, tired but contented.

These peaks are high-voltage. Yet we enjoy lower levels of spiritual energy every day, when we work on something we care about.

We need to increase our awareness of these four energies. Start by taking a deep breath. That gives more oxygen to your brain, so perception is enhanced. Take a quick 'energy audit' and notice how your body feels, what's going on in your mind, the emotions you are feeling and how connected you are to yourself and to others.

This needs practice. A great way is to set the timer on your mobile phone to alert you at twenty-minute intervals. When it buzzes in your pocket take a deep breath, sit straight and notice how your energies are. The more you do this the more energy-conscious you become throughout the day. The key is noticing when it's getting harder to be in the best place you can be.

That's when you need to act to change your state.

You are deliberately changing your state all the time. Think about what you do now when you get blocked or tired or bored. You might go for a walk, chat or get lunch (even if it's 11 a.m.). Everyone has their own little tricks.

One of the fastest ways to break a negative state is to take a deep breath, sit straight and smile.

The second fastest is to go somewhere else. Movement breaks your state and you get new stimulus. If that place is outside, it's double points.

Next time you find yourself not feeling quite right, losing your shine, breathe and check in. If your energies are out of kilter then do something, fast.

STAGE FRIGHT DELIGHT

I am often asked how to manage nervousness, especially when it comes to addressing meetings, making presentations or public speaking.

Nerves are your friends. I speak for a living and always have butterflies in my stomach and a rush of adrenaline before I step out in front of any group. It helps me to perform to a higher level.

I remember speaking at a conference when I seemed to have been on stage every day for a month. Eventually it all became so familiar that when I went out to speak I didn't have any jitters. I was lacklustre, I had no sparkle. I was hitting my marks in an unimpeachable but obviously professional way. Speaking had become so routine that I had lost my edge. Since then I have welcomed the nervous energy when it comes, because I know it's what I need to shine. We all need a little jitter, but we don't want it to take over to the extent that our hands become dancing puppets and our minds go blank. So what to do? Breathe. I mean really breathe. Most of us take tiny shallow breaths in the top half of our lungs. To really get some oxygen into your blood supply, your belly needs to expand just as a baby's would.

Stand up, put your hands on your tummy and make it push your hands outwards as the breath comes into your body. Without this breath your brain starves and starts to misbehave, just like an engine when it's running out of petrol.

Before standing in front of any group, breathe. And continue to breathe as you speak. It will help you pace your words and will feed your brain so that you can choose the right ones.

Next up, practise your first two minutes, know what

you're going to say and how you're going to say it, so you can relax. Visualize yourself speaking, looking confidently out from the stage and seeing the group looking back at you. Once you're in the flow your jitters will be gone, so just rehearse enough to get you feeling comfortable.

Be free to flow. Don't have a script and don't have lots of PowerPoint slides; they act like handcuffs. You are the show, not your visuals, so use slides only when they add real value. I use them as eye candy and none includes more than four words of annotation; mainly they are just pictures.

Be singular about the point you're trying to make. If you make too many, your audience will become confused and won't remember any of them. Be punchy and it will pay off.

Do something memorable that has humour and creates some interaction. If you get your audience to engage and you bring them into the conversation, it's much easier for you to be you rather than the 'presenter'.

Show yourself to be human early on. Years ago I was trained by a master at speaking who recommended starting a session in one of three ways: eating, drinking or laughing. They are things we all do and therefore connect the group to you subconsciously.

START BY TAKING A DEEP BREATH. THIS GIVES MORE OXYGEN TO YOUR BRAIN, SO PERCEPTION IS ENHANCED.

The principle is a good one. I get things wrong, I laugh at myself and I have been known to show pictures of myself in my underpants just to disarm the group and encourage them to engage with me as a person rather than a know-it-all adversary they may be inclined to shoot down.

The truth is, everyone wants you to perform well. Nobody is hoping that you screw up and have an embarrassing time. In fact they are hoping that you will shine and have fun while doing so, because then they'll have a better time themselves.

Personal agendas aside, your audience is always warm. They are always supportive of you being bigger, funnier and more compelling. That's why they're there.

Overcome the voices in your head by breathing deeply and keeping stuff simple, and you will always engage and delight. Just remember: it's your party – have fun.

DREAM YOUR WAY TO GENIUS

When we sleep, magical things happen. Although you may be away in La-La Land, unconscious of the workings of your brain, it's still doing wonderful things.

If you have ever woken up just before your alarm has sounded, you've experienced how precise your brain can be even when you are face down in a pillow.

Your brain is constantly processing, making sense of the day's stimuli and keeping your filing in order. Every night when you sleep the processing continues, which means that, if you're smart, you can have great ideas while dreaming.

Many enlightened inventors and rock 'n' roll thinkers have used sleep states to load the dice of their creativity. Edison, Dalí, Edgar Allan Poe and even Aristotle found the insights they gained in altered states an inspirational source.

We have to sleep every day to remain fit and well, so if we can use a part of our daily routine that requires no

WHEN WE **SLEEP,** MAGICAL THINGS HAPPEN.

effort to help us see things in new ways, we are literally living the dream; lazy man's genius.

The trick lies in understanding the portal to sleep. When we are in our usual functioning mode, running around, we only have access to our conscious brain. To get the magic we have to tap the subconscious, and the way we do that is by relaxing.

If you've ever lost something, then woken up knowing where it is, that's because you opened the portal to your subconscious brain. It has an extraordinary capacity for storing information and processes even as we snore.

So when you lie in bed you should relax down into that pillow, feel your muscles melting into the mattress and gently ponder the topic for which some creativity would be dandy. You are programming your subconscious so that it can work for you in your sleep.

When you wake, and have the first semblance of consciousness, write down whatever it is that you have in your mind.

It doesn't have to make any sense, just jot it down. Equally, if you wake in the night, do the same thing. If you do this every day for a week, you will find that the stuff you write begins to make more sense and becomes useful in cracking the opportunities around you. It does take some training, as you need to convince your subconscious that its fruits are valued, so you can make fruity idea pie.

The important thing is that you practise. Then every time you go to bed you have an opportunity to come back with gold … as well as some fine bed hair.

BELIEVE

People don't shine brightly unless they believe they deserve to do so.

You won't shine unless you believe it's right to do so.

Here's what internationally acclaimed spiritual teacher Marianne Williamson says about shining in her book *Return to Love*:

> *Our deepest fear is not that we are inadequate. Our deepest fear is that we are powerful beyond measure. It is our light, not our darkness that most frightens us.*
>
> *We ask ourselves, Who am I to be brilliant, gorgeous, talented, fabulous? Actually, who are you not to be? You are*

a child of God. Your playing small does not serve the world. There is nothing enlightened about shrinking so that other people won't feel insecure around you.

We are all meant to shine, as children do. We were born to make manifest the glory of God that is within us. It's not just in some of us; it's in everyone. And as we let our own light shine, we unconsciously give other people permission to do the same. As we are liberated from our own fear, our presence automatically liberates others.

The question is, where do these beliefs come from? They come from you and the sense you make of everything you experience. That quote may well have given you the jolt to reappraise your beliefs about why we're here, what holds us back and how we can be all we can be.

We collect evidence that supports our beliefs every day without even knowing about it. If you believe that you should shine – because it makes life so much more fun, will improve your business and ultimately make the world a better place to be – then you will. If you believe that within us all there is the potential to shine brightly, then your energy will pour forth.

Question is: what do you believe? Have a ponder.

Do you believe it's your duty to release your energy? Or are you scared of what might happen if you do, and instead just let it dissipate inside?

It's a big question. It's the only question.

You had the choice not to read this book, but you did. You have been trying different perspectives to see which ones fit and which are rightfully yours. By doing so, you have already set in motion a process of change.

You can now choose whether to continue that process or whether – as you might following an embarrassing one-night stand – you just take a long shower, hope no embarrassing rashes appear and pretend it never happened.

WHAT DO YOU BELIEVE?

SHINY ACKNOWLEDGEMENTS

I believe everyone can shine; everyone can stand out and be Elvis. I've witnessed it time and time again.

I can't mention everyone by name who has taught me that important lesson, or helped me believe in the good and the brilliance of humankind. But here's a few to whom I am indebted for helping me live what I believe (while loving every minute).

For real help on this book and beyond: My brother, Mark Brown, for his brilliance and endless support, Andy Fennell, Jo Foster, James Herring, Shilen Patel, Gordy Peterson, Jon Platt, Andy Reid and Paul Wilson. Thanks for your smarts, energy and gurudom. I owe you nice, if affordable, wine forever on.

To those who have always believed and created a world where I can do what I do: Rick Dzavik, Maria Eitel, Steve Fortune, Nicola Foster, Gretchen Heustis, Kevin Jackson, Nigel Martin, Susie Rixon, Sarah Severn, David Urquhart, John Van Vleck, Caroline Whaley and the mighty Keith Wilmot.

To my friends, co-conspirators and general forces for good: Suzi Stephenson, Coops, Tim Whaley, Kris Murrin, Rupert Millington, Mark Fowlestone, Tiny Thompson, Dave Allan, Jed Glanvill, Sean Jefferson, Matt Kingdon, David McCready, Ben Hall and Polly Steele, Jim Lusty, François Reynolds, Sticky, Steph and Matteo Ferrario, Maurice Duffy, Bad Boy Chris, the Tobeys and the Scudamores and the Bests, my grandfather Bill Woolmer (no cooler man ever walked this planet), my folks for always keeping faith and always humouring my latest evolution, Uma and Upa for being so Elvis in such a classy way and to all my old buddies at ?What If!

To the literati who made this happen, my editor, Joel Rickett, who always marked my homework with a smiley face, my copy-editor Trevor Horwood, who not only saved me from committing libel but made my writing so much better that my mother will think the education was all worthwhile, and my agent, Julian Alexander, who is a tireless champion and can always explain why the world is like it is. Thank you.

To Clodagh, Enzo and all my wonderful Blackbells around the globe.

My children, Harvey and Louli, who constantly remind

me that life is an adventure and that there is wonder all around. Priceless.

Finally, to all those who don't toe the line, those who are unreasonable with life and play it like the game it is; the ones who are true to themselves and never hide away. You make every day more Technicolor. You are Elvis, and because of you, business is a party.

<u>HOW DOES IT FEEL?</u>

Business can be extraordinary.

It can broaden your horizons and be rewarding and fulfilling.

It can excite, stimulate and help you become who you want to be.

But you have to want to play the game.

Only you can create your future. The bottom line is: how do you want it to look?

If you persist with what you're doing now, you can predict a linear existence. You will shine no more or less brightly than you do now, you will be no more or less successful than you are now, and all that will change is everything around you.

How does it feel? What's it like to be smaller than you can be, to achieve less than your

Chris Baréz-Brown is on a mission: to bring creativity, energy and engagement to the business world.

After helping turn Carling Black Label into the first British billion-pound brand, he joined ?What If!, the innovation and ideas agency. There he helped some of the world's biggest businesses get better at innovating.

In 2009 he founded Upping Your Elvis, a business whose sole focus is to release the genius of organizations by helping their people shine more brightly. He works with the likes of Coca-Cola, Nike and Citibank to help their teams make an extraordinary impact.

His previous book, *How To Have Kick-Ass Ideas*, was described as a 'champagne-in-the-veins tonic for jaundiced people' by Eden Project founder Tim Smit.

www.uppingyourelvis.com

potential, to accept today's reality rather than be unreasonable with the world around you?

If you feel great – well done, you. Get yourself another bag of Doritos, switch on the TV and enjoy your life.

If, however, you know you're here for a reason, and that reason is big and resonant and shiny, then you will take a huge bite out of this life regardless of what tries to slow you down.

You have everything you need to lead an exceptional life and to be a business exemplar.

You just need to turn up the volume, take off that professional mask and put on your dancing shoes. Then the party can begin.

Elvis lives in us all.

Go shine!